PENGUIN BOOKS
You're So Mummy

Alex Manson-Smith is a journalist and copywriter. She has written lifestyle features for *The Times, Telegraph, Guardian, Evening Standard* and *Observer*, as well as award-winning commercials for Google, YouTube and Nike.

Sarah Thompson is the author of *Style Council: Inspirational Interiors in Ex-Council Homes,* published by Random House in 2015. She's also a journalist and writes for the *Daily Telegraph* and *Prima Baby,* as well as for various commercial clients.

You're So Mummy

ALEX MANSON-SMITH
AND SARAH THOMPSON

MICHAEL JOSEPH
an imprint of
PENGUIN BOOKS

MICHAEL JOSEPH

UK | USA | Canada | Ireland | Australia
India | New Zealand | South Africa

Michael Joseph is part of the Penguin Random House group of companies
whose addresses can be found at global.penguinrandomhouse.com.

First published 2016
001

Copyright © Alex Manson-Smith and Sarah Thompson, 2016

The moral right of the authors has been asserted

Typeset by Palimpsest Book Production Limited, Falkirk, Stirlingshire
Printed in Great Britain by Clays Ltd, St Ives plc

A CIP catalogue record for this book is available from the British Library

ISBN: 978–1–405–92209–8

306.8743

www.greenpenguin.co.uk

Penguin Random House is committed to a
sustainable future for our business, our readers
and our planet. This book is made from Forest
Stewardship Council® certified paper.

For our own mums, Jan and Thelma.
Thank you doesn't really cover it.

Contents

Introduction

This isn't a book you can turn to for advice – or, in fact, any useful information about looking after your child. It's not going to tell you how to implement a routine or talk to them so that they will listen or get them into a good school. It's not going to give you any constructive help at all, to be honest. Having been through the gruelling early years, there are plenty of tips we could offer you (always carry raisins, don't believe people who say that babies can sleep in a drawer), but, frankly, you can get those from people better qualified than we are.

Although by rights we should be quite the experts. Between us we've read every parenting book going. We should know how to get babies to sleep and have tamed toddlers. Ours should be the calmest, easiest, happiest kids around. Except that we still don't feel any wiser. And often those books made us feel worse, because we never managed to carry out their advice properly.

And everything we read seemed to focus solely on the child. Who's pretty important, granted, but we also felt that we were undergoing some fairly epic changes ourselves. We wanted to read something that reflected that. There were books on motherhood, sure. But mostly they read like academic theses or else were full of go-girl high-fiving. Where were the books that talked the way we did, with all the swearing and moaning and unreasonable opinions?

We didn't want to outright gripe about motherhood – although it may sometimes appear otherwise, it's hands-down the best thing that's ever happened to either of us. But we wanted to acknowledge that bits of it can be a royal pain in the arse, and that you can love your children without always loving being a parent. We wanted to bring some honesty to motherhood, because it can feel like everyone's on a mission to sanctify the experience, which only makes a lot of us feel miserable and inadequate.

So in 2014 we started You're So Mummy (www.youreso mummy.com), which was really just a way for us to vent about how much we dislike baking, disguised as a blog. The feedback we had was so encouraging, we realized we'd hit a nerve and were inspired to write this book. We hope you enjoy it.

Sarah and Alex

Note: For simplicity's sake we use 'he' and 'husband' a lot when referring to partners/exes. That's not because we live in 1952 and think that every mother is married and straight, we promise. Please read this as code for significant other, whoever they are.

About Us

We met at school in Birmingham, aged eleven, bonding over our school shirts, which, instead of being regulation uniform, were from Next and had the alphabet printed on the pocket. We also both had a Marilyn Monroe cassette and knew all the words to 'Diamonds are a Girl's Best Friend'. From a love of 1980s retail and a Hollywood icon, great friendships grow.

Later on, we often visited one another at university, which we always found useful for getting off with each other's friends. We travelled a lot together in those days, although this was before young people went travelling to interesting places. Apart from a soggy camping trip to France that involved waking up with a taxidermy wallaby, most of our travels were conducted on the National Express. Today we're still each other's go-to companion for trips away, largely because we like doing the same things on holiday (drinking wine and going to Zara, only in a different country).

After graduating, we shared a mouldy flat in Islington above a shop called Jimmy's Shoes. The Jimmy Choo pun was lost on us at the time – which probably tells you all you need to know about how sophisticated our lives were.

Still, we had a lovely time, living out our ladette years peacefully on lager, cigarettes and recreational drugs. We often reminisce and laugh about how we might be dead now if we'd carried on. Halcyon days!

Eventually some kind men took pity and said they wanted to marry us, and we were thrilled to be one another's chief bridesmaid. Alex made Sarah dress up like a fat bloke from the office in a grey trouser suit, and Sarah made Alex look like one of the ladies from the Sheila's Wheels adverts, in a shiny green dress. We have fond memories of these special days, though both of us secretly enjoyed that afternoon on the terrace at Space in Ibiza in 2001 just ever so slightly more.

Life took us in different directions, and by the time we got around to having our first children we were living on opposite sides of the world. When Sarah had Stanley in 2006, she was in Bridport, Dorset, where she still lives. Three years later, when Alex had Emilio, she was in LA, where she wishes she still lived. So we haven't shared the experience of having children side by side – it's something we've gone through at different times and in different ways. Urban and rural-ish. Girls and boys. In an office, freelancing at home. Married and separated. Depressed and stupidly happy. Between us, we've covered all the bases.

When we get a minute, we both work as journalists and copywriters. Alex lives in Hackney with her husband, Misha, and their two sons. Sarah lives with her children in Bridport. We still try to snatch the odd weekend away, for drinking wine and going to Zara. Occasionally we even bring the kids along.

Oh yes, the kids. Sarah has Stanley, nine, and Betty, seven. And Alex has Emilio, six, and Xavier, three. They're about the funniest, cleverest and most beautiful kids in the world. Just like everyone else's kids.

Birth and Afterbirth

Getting hung up on a 'natural' labour

There are two big lies that women are sold during pregnancy: one, that it matters what kind of birth they have, and two, that this is something they can control. Health professionals are as much to blame as anybody else for this – after all, you'd think they'd have seen enough emergency C-sections to know that things don't always go as hoped.

But instead you're set up for a fall from day one. Newly pregnant, you skip off to your appointment with the midwife, who starts talking birth plans, and you come away with the impression that your labour experience is something you can order, like a takeaway ('I'll have one birthing pool, six scented candles and an Adele CD, please').

Eager to be an informed patient – and therefore in control – you hoover up books about pregnancy and childbirth, of which there are many. The big, medical-type ones aren't exactly a laugh a minute, and in fact read more like a list of terrifying outcomes – haemorrhaging, episiotomies, vaginal prolapses. So it's no wonder you find yourself drawn to the more gentle, female-centric books, which talk in terms of 'empowerment' and 'putting you at the centre of your own birth experience'.

Books like this offer the kind of comfort you want to hear, feeding you lines like 'childbirth only hurts if you're frightened'. And you clutch to this wisdom, sharing it with pregnant friends who are as wide-eyed and eager to believe it as you are. Your friends who are already mothers may laugh when you tell them this, but you put that down to jealousy because they didn't do enough research and it's too late for them now. You look into hypnobirthing and wonder if you might be one of those women you hear about – but strangely never meet – who find childbirth an orgasmic experience.

Even before you start birthing classes, you become your own little self-appointed expert on the subject. And the classes confirm what you've read, namely that if you do enough breathing exercises or slow dance with your partner or loll around on an exercise ball, your birth will be pain- and stress-free. A tiny part of you wonders why, if childbirth really is that easy, everyone makes such a massive hoo-ha about it, but you decide this is because the whole process is so medicalized these days that women aren't allowed to trust their own instincts. You may find yourself saying things like, 'Pregnancy is treated like an illness, when it's a perfectly natural state.'

You decide that an epidural isn't for you, because epidurals, like antidepressants, have been designated 'bad' drugs, even if you're a bit hazy on the whys of that. But other people keep telling you that you want to be present 'in the moment', not numbed and out of it on God-knows-what.

7

You may find that you haven't experienced this much peer pressure since your best friend in the second year talked you into having a perm. Friends who have drug-free births feel compelled to tell you as much afterwards, boasting that they had 'Nothing but a bit of gas and air!' You're not sure why it's good to suffer in childbirth though not with a headache, but it's enough to tell you that there's very much a 'right' way of doing this.

'Was it a natural birth?' people ask, the implication being, 'Was it a proper one?' It's even there in the language. Natural = good, wholesome, healthy, etc. Unnatural = strange, freakish, those Korean women who have so much plastic surgery they need certificates to get through passport control. It doesn't take a genius to work out which one you're supposed to plump for.

Some mothers can be downright sanctimonious about it, saying things like, 'I didn't want to do anything that would put my baby at risk.' This is a mean trick that puts you in a bit of a corner – after all, you can't go for the epidural now, can you? Not unless you're happy to *risk your newborn's health*, that is.

When the time comes, you arrive at the hospital, your bag packed, as ready as you'll ever be. The birth itself comes and goes, a mind-blowing whirl of agony, intensity, exhaustion and joy. But once the drama's over and things start to settle, you realize that, throughout all of this, you forgot one crucial thing – namely that childbirth is ten, maybe twenty hours of your life. If you come out of it not dead, you've done a great job.

And it dawns on you that everything the books and courses told you was bollocks, or at least not relevant to your particular experience. The breathing exercises – really? And exactly whose idea was the exercise ball? You wonder what the point was of that birth plan, the one that went out of the window about six hours in when you found yourself crouched naked over a chair, sweating and screaming for pain relief. The truth is, you could have gone in there knowing nothing and still achieved the same end result.

And you realize that all those hours you spent genning up on pregnancy and labour, you should have spent learning about babies and how to look after them. Because suddenly you've got one, and what on earth are you supposed to do with it now?

Wanting to be best friends with your midwife

Unless you are an avid vajazzler – and not counting sexytime, of course – the chances are you haven't spent many hours with a stranger rummaging around in your Mary. Throughout your pregnancy there will have been a bit of prodding and, if you're very lucky, a cervical sweep (when a woman you've never met comes round and fingers you right there on the sofa in broad daylight, to try and bring on labour).

So the midwife who sees you through childbirth is already quite a special person from the get-go. Even the lesbians among us are unlikely to have a woman in comfortable shoes spend so much time at the coalface in this lifetime (sorry, lesbians, for the comfy-shoes gag). But it's not just about the physical intimacy you share with this woman. You go through something with her – particularly if it is your first baby – that you will never go through with anyone else again, ever. And it feels so special to you that you think you must have found your new best friend.

Because even if you have the most intuitive birth partner in the world – one who says all the right things and doesn't, for example, play Warcraft while you writhe like a twat on a Swiss ball, or squeeze his spots in the bathroom mirror while you squirm like an eel in the bath (both real-life stories, reader) – the midwife nails it. She totally smashes it. If there was *The Voice* for midwives, the chairs would all spin round for her, not your rubbish birth partner, who has no stage presence and is wildly out of tune.

Whether you like her or not is an irrelevance – your connection to her is a visceral one. This woman knows how you feel at every moment of the hideous process. It's like she can read your mind. She holds your hand when they stick needles in you. She tells you you're amazing while simultaneously wiping away the poo from your backside. She shaves your pubes when it looks like you might have to have a C-section and, if you've had an epidural, she presses on your bladder to make you wee out of a straw. She stays on after her shift to see you through to the end, even though she has her own kids and it's the weekend, and she's been looking up your big old fanny for thirty-six hours now. She doesn't let it show that she thinks the names you have chosen are truly disgusting. She is a birth warrior, and you give yourself to her completely, a swooning Jane in her Tarzan-like grasp.

But, like anyone teetering up there on a pedestal of gas and air, she's liable to fall, this midwife of yours. She might make you think you're as special to her as she is to you, bringing you your lovely new baby all snuggly and wrapped-up and clean, and telling you what an amazing thing you've done. But beware – it's an obstetric honey-trap. She doesn't love you as much as you love her. You are just another notch on her bedpost. And when you come back to the ward to see her or she pops in to check your scar a few days later, she's nice and polite and everything – she really loves the box of Quality Street you bought her – but the spark has gone.

And you realize that she never really wanted to be your best friend at all – it's just her job to be a birth warrior. And you may ponder for a moment on the funny situation we western mothers find ourselves in during childbirth: legs wide open, stranger at the Mary. Because if this was the olden days (something that a certain type of middle-class mother likes to imagine quite often), she probably would have been your best friend or your mum or at least your aunty. But, on the other hand, you might have died in childbirth. Which makes you think about quite how privileged you are, but also how distant from this most natural of processes. Which, you don't appreciate at the time, is the last coherent thought you'll have for a while.

Giving your children creative names

Considering how much thought you've given it over the years, you'd expect that naming your children would be a breeze. So it's a surprise when you discover how hard it is, with the experience often ruined by the fact that you've got to take someone else's opinion into account. Usually this is a man who offers up no suggestions of his own, but responds to all yours by reminding you of some grim celebrity of the same name or by saying, 'I knew someone called that at primary school who was a right knob.'

This is annoying, because admitting the names you like takes courage. Most people are shy about their choices, simply because naming your child is such a public declaration of your tastes. Those unflattering jeans you bought, that hideous junk-shop chair – anything else you get wrong you can pass off as a hand-me-down or something you bought because it was cheap and you were premenstrual and not thinking straight. But your children's names are a decision you have to stand by, even if you were drunk at the time or going through a phase where you thought it would be really cool to name them after one of the planets.

These days your children's names are a statement of Who You Are, which forces you to decide exactly that. This is fine if you're the old-school posh type as you can just pick something strong and traditional. Similarly, it must be easy if you're religious or have a hero or family member you want to name them after. In fact, the problems only really start if you've got yourself down as the creative type. Because, as a creative type, you're not allowed to give your child a nice name – the reason being that, if it's a nice name, other people will have gone for it too. Which means that it will be (horror) a popular name. And as a creative person, the last thing you can do is give your kid the same name everyone else has. Ideally you're looking for something as unique as they are – something that will make everybody else feel annoyed and jealous that they didn't think of it first. Which is how you come to find yourself scouring the baby-name dictionary for the 68,000th time, wondering whether Sinbad has a nice ring to it.

Friends and family tend to make the whole thing even harder. The weight of expectation is upon you, with loved ones waiting for you to conjure something that's original and inspired, without being downright weird. Apart from 'What are you having?' and 'When are you due?', 'Thought of any names yet?' is about the only thing you're asked during pregnancy, and by your twentieth week you've had enough of it. 'Yes, but we're not telling anyone,' you snap. Or, if you're nicer than that: 'Nope, still arguing about it!' Later it dawns on you that they were probably just trying to make conversation, but at the time it only adds to the pressure.

That said, sharing your ideas for names with anyone but your partner is a mistake. Whoever you tell either falls about laughing or, worse still, is polite, damning your choices with a hesitant 'Ye-*es*' or 'How unusual!' Those closest to you come right out and say it: 'You can't call him that – think of the shit he'll get in the playground!' If they really want to piss on your parade, they say something like, 'Oh, I think there's a Kardashian with one of those . . .'

But as the creative mother soon learns, twenty-first-century playgrounds are chock-full of Lovedays, Gustavs and Indigos. Which is when it dawns on her that, if she'd really wanted to be different, she should have called him Paul.

The rules of creative naming

Creative people like to give the impression they plough their own furrow, but really there's a code as rigid as royal protocol. Not just any old weird or made-up name cuts it – there are rules:

1. Under no circumstances can you name your child after a flower (too popular) or a city (too common). Animals, however, are fair game: Fox, Wolf, Bear, Otter – these are all entirely acceptable first names. See also the natural world and weather: River, Cloud, Rainbow.

2. Haven't read a classic novel since school? Never mind. Just plunder your GCSE set texts for ideas. *To Kill a Mockingbird* in particular is a winner. Atticus, Scout, Harper – these tell the world you've read a book *and* are anti-racist. Alternatively, try one of the Ts, like Tennyson or Tennessee. Eager to prove you read outside the syllabus? Try Hunter or Huxley. Aesthetes and romantics can plunder the Victorian texts and Thomas Hardy: Dorian, Bathsheba, Virginia, etc.

3. To prove your anti-establishment credentials, give them a name that sounds like it belonged to a criminal or, at the very least, someone clinically insane, e.g. Sid, Ted, Jonny, Harold. Fred and Rose is perfect for twins.

4. Alternatively, subvert suspicions about your privileged upbringing by giving them a name so

outrageously posh it can only be a joke: Monty, Rupert, Clarence, Ludo, etc.

5. You can show your disdain for convention with an obscure Biblical name. Clearly Matthew, Mark, Luke and John aren't going to pass muster here. But Hephzibah? Heber? Go for your life.

6. If you are white, give them a soul name: Otis, Elwood, Billie, Aretha, etc.

7. If you dress your children like evacuees and make them play with vintage toys, try your local cemetery or bingo hall for inspiration, e.g. Edith, Ethel, Stan, Betty.

8. Failing that, you can opt for the surname as first name, e.g. Beckett, Miller, Bailey (NB the name must belong to some 1960s artist type – this isn't going to work with, say, Cruikshank or Butt). This was good enough for Stella McCartney and she's cool, right? Talking of which:

9. If you're feeling insecure about your choices, you can fall back on something with the celebrity stamp of approval. Name your child Lila, Ramona, Rudy or Finlay and you can draw comfort that Jude Law, Kate Moss and Maggie Gyllenhaal did the same. But be warned, this is a cop-out and you will be judged accordingly.

10. Ideally you will pick something outside of the Top 100 Most Popular Baby Names. If your choice is in the Top 50, then clearly you have failed. But if it starts low and moves up the list next year, then five points to you – you have started a trend.

11. If you've got heritage, make the most of it. Great-grandparents on one side were Irish? Great, you've got an Aoife or an Oisín.

12. If your own heritage is too mundane, feel free to steal someone else's. Your experience of Spanish culture might amount to no more than a childhood trip to Fuengirola and a week in Ibiza you can't remember, but this is no barrier to naming your offspring Carmen or Emilio. However, be sure to check medical dictionaries for possible mishaps. See: *Melina* (pretty Latina girl's name) and *Melena* (black, tarry faeces associated with gastrointestinal bleeding).

Wishing you hadn't bothered with NCT

Like many things you only discover once you're knocked up (who'd ever heard of Braxton Hicks or knew that bodybuilders drink colostrum, the sickos?), you'd never heard of NCT before babies. Even now, you're not actually sure what it stands for: Natural Childbirth Trust? National Childbirth Trust? National Charity for Trust in Childbirth? Wah?

But when we get pregnant, we overly conscientious women tend to launch ourselves on to a gestatory conveyor belt, stacked high with Things We Do (and Don't Do), in order to produce the Best Baby Ever. These include, but are not limited to: pregnancy yoga, pregnancy massage, any kind of alternative therapy with the word pregnancy prefixing it, wearing inadequate bras, overdosing on rooibos and removing all fun from the diet. We take this last one so ser-iously that we actually stop drinking alcohol (even though our own 1970s mothers swigged warm hock every night over the cheesy leeks) and caffeine (even though they glugged Mellow Birds from the moment they woke up, a vision in polyester).

Some of us take the self-flagellation with a bigger pinch of salt than others – the truly reckless among us may even eat the occasional prawn sandwich. But one activity we all seem to flock to unquestioningly is NCT. It's a sort of ology pre-parents feel they must pass in order to be truly pregnant. It's the Cycling Proficiency of childbirth. And you sign up for it without really thinking about why; you just know that everyone does it 'for the friends you make' and something about epidurals being bad.

So it is that, some weeks later, you and your partner find yourselves in the local Quaker Meeting House, watch-ing a woman with hairy, Frodo-like toes (you know this because she is not wearing any shoes) pull an old Tiny Tears doll with no eyes through a giant plastic vagina. Glancing around at your fellow classmates, you identify the couple whose faces are also streaming with silent tears of laughter. And, *ta-da*, you have found your fabled NCT friends.

With hindsight you realize that you should just have got Fun Couple's number and not gone back. But hindsight's a bugger like that, always showing up late. So instead you return like pregnant zombies to another six weeks of natural-birth night school, drinking herbal teas with Frodo and sharing visualization strategies for coping with con-tractions ('imagine you are surfing a wave'). You watch a live breastfeeding demonstration by a woman who, the guy from Fun Couple speculates, gave birth in a field, assisted by a vet.

You spend a lot of time rotating your pelvis on a core ball while your partner looks on awkwardly (the closest you ever get to the real birth experience). And you play confusing games with pebbles, designed to drive home the message that pethidine is arsenic for babies and that epidurals are responsible for most problems in the western world.

Then it all happens and it's like the end of *One Flew Over the Cuckoo's Nest* when Jack Nicholson gets his lobotomy. Resistance was futile. You had every medical intervention there is and your birth plan was no more helpful than that stupid sodding TENS machine. The soothing playlist you curated was drowned out by the crowd of students gathered around your back end, and the surfing visualization strategies were as effective as drinking water upside down to cure hiccups.

Years later, cosied up with your old friend hindsight again, you realize that, despite having an epidural and giving your baby formula milk, you and the child are both fine. And you see that NCT, while its heart is probably in the right place, is mostly another way for women to make themselves feel inadequate. And you wish you hadn't taken it all so bloody seriously. But at least you can still piss yourself laughing about the giant plastic vagina while getting shitfaced with Fun Couple.

Bjorn v Ergo: Defining
yourself through baby brands

You probably don't think of yourself as the kind of woman to fall for branding. When it comes to Persil *v* Ariel or Evian *v* Volvic, chances are you couldn't care less. You're happy to buy the supermarket own-brand label if it means saving money. You're too sophisticated for the marketing bullshit.

Except when it comes to buying baby gear. Then what should be as simple as buying whatever's cheapest and/or best suddenly becomes imbued with all kinds of subtext. Take something as seemingly straightforward as a baby carrier. This should be nothing more than a simple means of transporting your child from A to B. There are several types available, all providing pretty well the same function. Yet each sends out a very different message to the world.

Buy a wrap sling and the world has you pegged as a professional breastfeeder, all homeopathic teething powders and strongly held opinions on baby-led weaning. The Ergobaby, meanwhile, is for those who still consider themselves of the eco persuasion, but like to think of themselves as a bit trendy with it. The Baby Bjorn, the traditional choice of south-west London types, is the smartest and most established of the three. But, like the Bugaboo, its pushchair equivalent, the Bjorn has a tendency to come over as smug and privileged, irritating as many people as it appeals to. It's a trap that befell poor Boden, which, despite making attractive, functional, well-priced clothes, managed to make the whole country want to smack it in the face.

The marketeers are clever. They know that you 'only want the best for your child'. They also know that you are tired and hormonal and, given only the tiniest encouragement, will fork out for all manner of shit. Which explains how there came to be a market for changing bags and bottle warmers, bath thermometers and baby-food blenders – all entirely unnecessary products.

The marketeers also know they can create desires where there were none. Who would have known you could hanker after a particular brand of muslin? But Aden & Anais had the ingenuity and foresight to know that, if they printed giraffes on them, you would pay 500 per cent over the odds for a small square of cloth.

Not that you'd ever admit you were suckered by marketing. Instead you tell yourself that, having done your research, you can now confidently say that Maxi-Cosi makes the best car seats and UPPAbaby the best buggies. This is why you want them. Not because they're the ones you fancy the look of. Oh no. Instead it's all about quality and functionality. You can even tell yourself it's about *your baby's health*, after you read somewhere that *insert name of undesirable brand here* will stunt your baby's growth and leave it with hip dysplasia.

Marketing is the reason that everybody ends up (though seldom starts) with a Maclaren. Because Maclaren, despite making perfectly decent buggies that don't cost a month's salary, comes across as a bit boring and hausfrau. Practical though it is, the Maclaren is not 'lifestyle'. Unlike the Baby Jogger City, it doesn't reassure you that you're still a hip girl about town. It doesn't say you can afford to spunk the best part of a grand on a buggy. It says that you've given up and turned into your mum. This may be why such a lot of new mothers start with something bigger and shinier, before realizing they'd actually like to be able to manoeuvre their way around cafes and trading it in for a Techno XT.

The baby products you buy give you membership to a tribe. Unfortunately, this can be one you don't want to join. Which is perhaps why so many mothers who go for the 'prestige' brands end up endlessly apologizing about it afterwards. 'It was a bargain on eBay,' they lie, or, 'We only got it cos they hold their value so well.'

As always, the best solution is to inherit someone else's stuff. Then you'll gratefully take whatever you get. It also gives you your get-out-of-jail-free card. That way, no one can infer anything from your Stokke cot – after all, you were given it.

Failing at sleep training

On the really bad days you feel like one of Monty Python's Yorkshiremen – like you got up before you went to bed – and can't actually imagine what it's like to have a full, uninterrupted night's sleep. These are the days when no amount of Clarins Double Serum can hide the fact that you've aged ten years, and the smallest setback has you fantasizing about a short spell in a psychiatric ward, where at least you'd be left on your own for a bit. This is when you admit you've hit breaking point and that Something Must Be Done.

Tempting though it is, one of the worst things you can

do in this situation is confide in people. Because, in this situation, friends tend to do one of two things. They may say something like, 'Gosh, we're really lucky like that, Ava's always been a good sleeper. Sometimes we have to actually wake *her* up!' Alternatively, they start giving you advice about sleep training. This is well meant but annoying, as it assumes that you know nothing about it, when in fact you've spent a short epoch Googling it and could now sit an A level in the subject. They foist books on you, which you don't want because you already have three and surely that's got to be enough.

But you are desperate and teary, and when you admit your child's sleeping patterns, friends bite their bottom lips and look aghast, as if they've never heard of such a thing. This makes you feel even more of a failure and like the problem is your parenting, not the fact that you've got a tiny sadist on your hands who thinks that 4.30 a.m. is an A-OK time to start the day.

So you resolve to sleep train. This isn't an easy decision as you have half the internet telling you that you are EVIL and your baby will be psychologically scarred for life. Your friendship group is equally divided, with some having had theirs in a routine from day one, and the others swearing they could never let a baby cry. They each make you feel bad, because you have managed to both let your baby cry *and* failed to get them into any kind of sleeping pattern.

But the pro-sleep trainers gee you up, telling you that a bit of crying will do them no harm, especially when the alternative is a depressed mother. And what use will you be to your child when you lose your job? Huh? HUH???

You feel yourself moving off the fence and on to team routine, and resolve to get started on sleep training that night.

But having read so much about it, you start to get the details confused. So you're supposed to go in every five minutes – you've got that. But what happens if they're still crying? Are you allowed to leave? Or do you just sit there, cooing at them through the cot bars until they calm down? You shudder, knowing how long that could take. And it's all very well making these plans during the day, but at 3 a.m., when they're screaming and you don't think your brain or the neighbours can take it any more, it's got to be easier just to chuck a bottle of milk in the cot and run.

Come 3 a.m., it turns out that this is totally the easier option. Naturally it also turns out to be the absolute worst thing you can do. Because not only have you endured a night of anxious crying – and that's just you – you're also back at square one on the sleep training.

And now that you've tried it, you start to dwell on the what-ifs. What if you have broken the sacred bond of trust between mother and child and they never forgive you? What if it's true that leaving them to cry floods their brain with cortisol, making them stressed and aggressive in later life? What if your placid little baby turns out to be a psychopath and it's *all your fault*?

At three in the morning you can find yourself getting quite dramatic about it all. But, as usual with these things, your children will have the last laugh, emerging unscathed and oblivious. And eventually you too will come to laugh at your unnecessary angst in the same way that you will laugh at yourself for thinking it was important to have a nappy bag, and that eating salad during pregnancy would result in a child who liked vegetables. By this point you won't remember what the exhaustion felt like, any more than you can remember what toothache feels like.

But you will have been through it, which qualifies you as an expert in the field. So when friends with babies come to you, hollow-eyed and tearful, unable to remember when they last slept properly, you get to tell them exactly what they need to do.

Trying to save the planet via our offspring

Perhaps one of the most powerful urges that besets today's new parent is the need to save the planet. It must be a survival thing. After all, it's a terrifying prospect: bringing a child into the world, when you're not actually sure how much longer the world is staying open. It's only natural we should want to fight to keep the party going, like disappointed drunks who've missed last orders.

Most of us have already bought into the concept of eco-living before we get pregnant anyway. We do the recycling and switch off when we leave the room. We buy Ecover washing-up liquid (largely because it looks nicer by the sink than the others, but we don't tell anyone that), we have a frumpy organic T-shirt from People Tree and two pairs of bamboo socks. We are only a falafel away from being actual Linda McCartney.

But once those little blue lines appear, an alarm goes off and it's all hands on green deck. Nine months of baby growing gives us a chance to really think about how we are going to patch up the ozone and re-grow the coral.

In the face of some pretty massive eyebrow raising and *just you wait* faces from our parents, and friends who have already tried, unsuccessfully, to save the planet via their own offspring, we announce our eco intentions to the world. Not for us those handy disposable nappies and scented bags, so wasteful and synthetic with their Disney characters and moisture-wicking ways.

We'll be washing all our nappies by hand, using only lemon juice and vinegar – we may even say the term 'nature's cleansers' out loud. No chemically-bleached-and-dyed babygros for our zygotes, we'll be dressing mini-Swampy in organic bamboo onesies and non-gender-specific stars and stripes. We'll be drenching them in oils: brushing their teeth with coconut oil, soothing their nappy rash with lavender oil, making their hair look greasy with unspecified 'natural' oils. And they will only be playing with earth-friendly wooden rattles. As for evil life-saving vaccines? Haven't you heard about those amazing amber necklaces? DUH.

Sure, it's worth being environmentally conscious during the baby years – man, we get through some product – but it can seem like another form of self-harm for the already overwhelmed postnatal mother. Hey, you guys, let's not think about the fact that we're about to spend the next three years awake, with someone else's poo under our fingernails. Let's focus instead on making life even harder with ineffectual products, extra housework and snubbing anyone whose baby whiffs of Johnson's, the devil's own bubble bath (as any eco parent knows). It's no surprise that those who keep it up full-time, cycling every-where in hareem pants and burying their placentas under trees willy-nilly, can seem a little sanctimonious, or else plain miserable.

Most of us lesser beings end up doing a half-arsed eco-effort. We give the washables a go but eventually decide we can't cope with the massive backside they give our beautiful baby. We then flit between Nature nappies and Lidl's own brand, caught in a never-ending tug of war between being green and being cheap. We try making our own wipes with witch hazel and that Castile soap that costs more than a decent Pinot, but given the choice between sleeping and making our own baby wipes, we choose life. We buy the organic baby-food pouches by the trolley load, putting into the recycling bin of our mind the fact that they have been pasteurized to oblivion and have a sell-by date that's after our baby's first day at big school. We do all these half-arsed things and more because, frankly, it's too exhausting being green. We'll have to save the planet another day.

Baby yoga, Gymboree and Kindermusik: pissing away your maternity leave

Hooray, maternity leave. A time to wander the shops, drink flat whites and read magazines, maybe with the odd jaunt to an art gallery thrown in. At least, that's what it should be. Unfortunately, what it really ends up being is a punishing time of sleep deprivation, guilt and way too much cake.

It's a shame, really. Because unless you're lucky enough

to be wildly rich, this may well be your first extended period without work. So you'd think you might be able to enjoy it – to really make the most of this time out, which you may never be lucky enough to experience again. But no.

In part this is down to the challenges that you bring on yourself. It's the demon voice on your shoulder, the one telling you that if you were a proper mother, you wouldn't be sitting in ancient tracksuit bottoms, mainlining biscuits. You would be doing baby massage and Kindermusik and baby yoga, even though you're inclined to do none of these things and, in truth, aren't even sure what baby yoga is. Who does the yoga? Can a baby do a sun salutation?

Your sensible side will tell you that these activities are a waste of money and will have precisely no impact on your child's long-term prospects. They're ridiculous, you tell yourself – invented by a cynical baby industry and other mothers who need a job with easy hours. But overriding this is your crazy, hormonal side, which tells you that, by not doing these things, you are doing your child a dis-service. You start catastrophizing, foreseeing situations where your eight-year-old drowns on holiday because you couldn't be bothered to take him to baby swimming.

And it's hard to resist that postcard on the community board advertising lessons in your neighbourhood. Yes, they're expensive. Yes, they're probably pointless. But it might be a chance to meet like-minded women, now you've learned that pushing a buggy around the park, staring after other mothers you like the look of, probably isn't the best way to make new friends.

So you haul yourself to the class, cursing yourself for

having made a commitment to be somewhere at a particular time when it takes you the best part of a morning to brush your teeth. And, sure enough, the class manages to be both boring *and* stressful. Your baby would rather be at home, feeding. You would rather be asleep. You make no friends.

After that comes the guilt: guilt that you're spending too much money on classes and coffees. Guilt that you promised to visit your friend twenty miles away, but feel weirdly anxious about getting in the car with the baby. Guilt that, because you're not working, you should be making fabulous meals from scratch and keeping a tidy home, even though there aren't enough hours and you don't remember signing up to be that person anyway.

There's also the guilt about not being more productive with your time. This is fed by an irritating stream of articles about 'mumpreneurs' who, during their maternity leave, set up businesses from their kitchen table. Justine Roberts set up Mumsnet after she had her first baby. Why haven't you set up Mumsnet? Because you're too busy staring, slack-jawed, at the clock, wondering how the hell it can still be only 9 a.m., that's why.

Then your baby will get older, and you really will have to start doing the rounds of swimming and soft plays, the activities designed solely for their entertainment. And you'll wish you'd spent those early months doing what you should have been doing all along – namely, absolutely bugger all.

Finding a parenting guru

When you have your first baby, one of the many crap jokes people like to make is, 'They don't come with a manual!' Ah, you think, but that's where you're wrong. I have bought this tome by Penelope Leach/Gina Ford/some crazy American hippie* (*delete as appropriate) and she is my guiding light. She will show me the way.

These books may differ in their approaches, but they essentially amount to the same thing, which is bossy women with an opinion telling you what to do. Admittedly, what with your mother and mother-in-law, you're not exactly short on those. But your mother and mother-in-law don't always tell you what you want to hear. They come with their own ideas, fresh from the 1970s, which they like to push on you by pursing their lips or sighing every time you try and do anything they don't approve of.

So what you really want is an expert to validate your already entrenched views on child-rearing. This gives you ammunition, so that when your mother/mother-in-law starts telling you what's wrong with your approach, you can come back with, 'Well, the Baby Whisperer says . . .' In other words, it's not you telling her to bog off and leave you alone, it's the Baby Whisperer. An *authority*.

Although, to be fair, you could do with the advice these books offer, too. Because, though many grannies are generous with their opinions, they're not always so forthcoming with the useful nuts and bolts. Some think it's enough to stand around saying, 'I don't know why your generation are so hung up on "designer" buggies – a fold-up Maclaren was fine for us.' Or, 'Don't ask me, I can't remember, I think we just shut you in a room.' Otherwise they do you no favours by living miles away and having a diary Hillary Clinton would want to think about trimming back.

So you may find that it's just you and the book. In the early days, you keep it close to hand, referring to it if your baby so much as farts. Some helpfully offer daily timetables, which tell you what you should be doing at any given moment of the day. The danger here is that you allow these to rule your life, collapsing into meltdown if you find yourself forty minutes off schedule ('That's it, the day's screwed!'). You berate yourself for oversleeping when your day was supposed to start at 7 a.m., even though it didn't seem to end at all, and get into a massive panic about whether it's OK to feed your baby at 11 a.m. if the book says it should be 11.15 a.m.

Often your friends have picked their own baby gurus to follow, and if you've chanced upon the same one it gives you a common bond that lets you feel you've got one over acquaintances who've chosen other, lesser gurus. Some friends, however, may meet your lyrical endorsements with judgemental silence or pointed comments along the lines of, 'Oh, you do it like that, do you?' or, 'I reckon people should just do whatever works for them.' You may find that baby gurus are one of those subjects, like money and politics, that are best avoided altogether.

Of course, it can be tempting to switch horses and buy a different book just because your friend has it. After all, her baby seems way more placid than yours – maybe the book is the reason. And at £6.99, it's got to be worth a shot. But the risk here is that you confuse yourself, bouncing between enforcing a routine and responding to your baby's every gurgle, and failing at both.

It pays to be careful, because parenting books can be addictive. You can find yourself accumulating a shelf-full of them. This is because, as with dieting, reading about parenting is a fat lot easier than actually parenting.

In any case, the more parenting books you read, the more you start to see how much they contradict each other. Somebody's got to be wrong, you think. And so the seeds of doubt are sown. What if it's all bollocks? What if . . . *no one knows anything*? What if your dad was right, and you should stop buying all these stupid manuals and read something interesting instead?

And suddenly you've seen the wizard behind the curtain. You are over your guru. You don't need her any more. You can cock up all by yourself, thanks. And just knowing this is intensely liberating. So you thrust the books on some poor pregnant friend who'd been hoping for the Caramel Baby & Child cashmere cardi, and free up some valuable shelf space. Which you can start filling with books about how to get the most out of primary school.

So Long, Farewell, *Auf Wiedersehen*, Goodbye: Your Mental Health

Popping the pills

In the early weeks after childbirth, health professionals sniff around with multiple-choice questionnaires about the baby blues and how often you cry, and are you at all interested in committing suicide?

This concern is nice, but seems kind of arbitrary when you're busy having your tits collapsed by the small vampire they wrenched out of your tattered vagina, and wondering if it will be OK to serve ham sandwiches again for tea. Even if you had the brain cells to think straight, you're not going to admit to finding things tough at this early stage in the game, are you? You're armed and ready with the Gina Ford collection and a baby bath. What could possibly go wrong?

Really they should sniff around about two years later. Because this is when the baby blues kicks in. When you've realized that the man you had the babies with can only do household chores if they come with calligraphed instructions and full sex as a reward. You've been under house arrest, on half-rations of sleep, for twenty-four months.

You have the sense that you've suffered a profound trauma – one that, paradoxically, you wouldn't change. So it's now that you begin to crumble.

It starts small. Leaving the house, you wonder, did you turn off the iron? Just pop back and check. You leave the child in the buggy outside, and worry so much in those few moments that someone will swoop in and steal her, that you don't register checking the iron (it was off). Fifty paces down the road you stop, then go and check again, because you really need to know the iron is off. Visions of towering infernos and your neighbours being carried out in body bags flash through your mind.

Little things begin to taunt you. Someone you know drives past and doesn't wave. Why didn't they wave? They must dislike you. A friend you were hoping to meet for coffee doesn't text you back. Oh right, so they don't like you, either. And come to think of it, you haven't heard from your sister in a while. Clearly, everybody hates you.

The paranoia starts to take over your life. You put your daughter down for her afternoon nap – an hour of peace. But you check on her (to make sure she's not dead) so many times, you completely waste this chance to rest. You begin to avoid driving anywhere if you can, as you've lost your nerve on the roads. Driving at any speed above stationary has come to represent little more than a series of narrowly missed accidents. Public transport is no better – on train platforms you pin yourself to the wall or grip the platform seats to stop yourself falling on the line (or is it from throwing yourself on?). Don't even mention planes. Who travels on a plane – a metal box in the sky – once they've had children? You are Edvard Munch's *The Scream* brought to life.

One day, as you take the scissors from the top of the fridge (where you have hidden them, with the knives, to prevent accidents), you tell your sister why they are there, and she says, *This isn't normal, girl. Give yourself a break. Antidepressants might help.* 'Pah!' you reply. 'I'm not depressed. Look at me, I'm all up and dressed and ready to go about my daily activities! I laugh in the face of antidepressants.' And you say some other stuff about having to go through the lows to feel the highs and not wanting to take medication – as if feeling bad is somehow cleverer.

But the suggestion lingers. The promise of release from your twisted state is alluring. You know you're not yourself any more. And you kind of miss your old self, with her freedom and lightness of spirit. So you decide to look into the pills.

Online you find forums full of desperate-sounding women, asking when they will start working. Knowing replies urge them to keep going, they will soon kick in and all will be well. Others talk of sleepless nights and vivid dreams, palpitations and night sweats. Some say they can't have orgasms. You learn this is a major side effect of taking antidepressants, and it strikes you that here is a cruel irony – to feel normal again you have to sacrifice the one free kick at your disposal. Like the Little Mermaid when she sells her soul, you can have your legs but we'll keep your voice, thank you.

It turns out that antidepressants aren't just for depression. They're widely prescribed for anxiety, premenstrual disorder, panic attacks and eating disorders, too. One in three women in the UK take antidepressants at some point in their lives. Blimey, that's a lot. Come to think of it, you do know quite a few women who are on them. Loads, actually.

You do a quick headcount of the mum friends you know who've used them. There's the one who doesn't love her husband but stays for the kids, and the one who's been out of work so long she's lost her confidence. There's the mother coping with special needs, and the one who works way too much but can't afford not to. It wouldn't be an overstatement to say that more than half the mothers you know are, or have been, propping up their mental health with pills.

Maybe you should do yoga? Eat more superfoods? For every article about antidepressants there's one about how exercise can help, or how to eat yourself happy. But as far as solutions go they seem kind of inadequate at this stage. A Mr Bump plaster for someone with a broken leg.

Meditation, mindfulness, Cognitive Behavioural Therapy. You learn all about these things. They sound more like it – you'll give them a go. But NHS waiting lists for CBT are long, and going private costs the sort of money you should probably be spending on the mortgage instead. Mindfulness meditation helps – you get Headspace on your phone, you learn to breathe. But it's a practice that requires focus and time, dedication and commitment. All of which you are lacking, what with the chronic anxiety and children under five.

Eventually the promise of relief becomes irresistible and you go to your GP and sob in his chair – and it's as simple as that. He's not surprised. It's very common, everyone is under such a lot of strain. Nothing to be ashamed of. Perfectly safe. Next please.

Four weeks later, you're cooked to perfection. Wonderfully carefree and deliciously blithe. When your husband wants to have a domestic, you just laugh. If the kids don't want to get dressed, that's fine. Work a bit full-on? You sign up for overtime. You are enjoying life. You can do it at last. And you wonder why you didn't go on them sooner and tell everyone how good they are and drive everywhere like a maniac and never think about the iron again – woo-hoo!

But each morning when you take your pill you remember, for a brief moment, what is happening here. And it occurs to you that it's quite a sorry state of affairs, really. That we twenty-first-century women can't cope with the situation we've found ourselves in. We're messing with our brain chemistry, just so we can effect some sort of version of being normal. It would actually be quite a big thing to think about, and would probably make you feel sad.

But right now you feel good, so you're not going to go there.

Going mental over schools

You can't say you didn't see it coming. Friends with older children were the canaries down the mine, and you watched as they turned from being normal-ish people with a variety of interests into insane obsessives capable of discussing only one subject.

You'd make the mistake of letting the conversation drift in the direction of schools, only to endure an agitated monologue along the lines of, 'I mean, the Ofsted reports aren't even right half of the time. They're obsessed with things like how often they wash their hands. It's ridiculous.' *I know*, you'd nod, trying not to die of boredom.

Other friends went even madder, finding Jesus exactly two years before the application deadline. And how you enjoyed judging them for it. You'd never go that far, you thought. I mean, the hypocrisy of it. You'd hear of people paying way over the odds to rent in the vicinity of such-and-such a school that's so popular the catchment is only 150 metres!

There was no way you'd behave like that, you'd tell yourself – you were way too chilled. Besides, you didn't have to think about schools for, like, five years. By which time you'd be so rich you could pack them off to that place in Notting Hill where Claudia Schiffer and Stella McCartney's kids go, so they could have cute uniforms for the end-of-year photo and be bezzie mates with the Beckham children.

Only, cut to five years later and, having spunked untold amounts of cash on childcare and bad camping trips, you're even worse off than you were before. Not only that, but you've discovered how much these private schools actually charge. Never mind the fees, you can't even afford the *Good Schools Guide* (Forty quid? Who are they kidding?).

Meanwhile, your nearest primary has 'challenges', no uniform at all and a playground that looks like the set of *Orange is the New Black*. But not much further away there's a C of E school that gets brilliant results at Key Stage 2 – whatever that is – and made it on to one of those lists the *Sunday Times* goes in for.

And you realize that the devil might have the best tunes, but God's bagsied the schools. So you torment yourself about whether you're doing your child a disservice by not finding Jesus, while railing to anyone who'll listen about the ridiculousness of the system ('But NO ONE under sixty is Christian in this country! I mean, even in mad old America, they know to separate school and religion, right?').

And when you glance at the person you're talking to for validation, you spot a familiar look in their eye – one that screams, 'HELP ME,' as they nod sympathetically and say, 'I know.'

Loony on toast: Losing it over food

Our mothers had it so easy. Back in the eighties, feeding your kids was a simple affair: Frosties, fish fingers, Ritz crackers with a squirt of Primula cheese on top – all washed down with a Feast and a carton of Um Bongo. Those were the days when Mars bars were marketed as healthy, and no one even thought to take issue with children's sweets that looked like fags.

Had organic food been around then, eighties mum would have held no truck with it. ('What, so it's like normal fruit, only more expensive and bashed-about looking?') She was too busy enjoying novelty ice-cream toppings ('It pours as a liquid, but sets when it touches the ice cream!') and the time-saving qualities of her microwave.

When it came to food, the bar back then was lower. Go

to a restaurant – even a swanky one – and the choice of starters alone was enough to tell you that this was a decade with convenience on its mind: a slice of melon, topped with ground ginger; frozen prawns, doused in a mixture of ketchup and mayo; orange juice, for heaven's sake.

Then, suddenly, in the late 1990s – at about the time we discovered balsamic vinegar and sun-dried tomatoes – the game changed and food became a thing. Obviously there were advantages to this, as anyone who grew up on tinned peaches topped with Carnation milk will tell you. And as a nation we discovered cooking, or, more accurately, watching other people cook on TV.

British food went from being an international joke to being actually pretty good. Which was fine – great, even – but, as we did with the drinking, we had to take it too far. It wasn't enough to have a few decent restaurants and gastropubs. Instead we had to go full foodie, with blogs and YouTube channels, pop-ups and supper clubs.

Nowadays you can't buy a newspaper without a great fat recipe supplement falling out. These are basically a massive guilt trip, designed to make you feel bad for not cooking saffron risotto cakes and rhubarb cobbler for your family. Because you needed something else to beat yourself up about.

Practically the only thing we see more of than food porn is obesity statistics. A third of our children are too fat. For the first time they're going to have shorter life expectancies than our own. The fear this creates is pervasive. Your child might be the proverbial rake, but now he can barely eat an ice cream without you mentally flashing forward to him aged eighteen, and forty-two stone, being craned out of your living-room window. Is he eating too much junk, you wonder? And how much is too much, anyway?

The trouble is, you then risk going too far the other way. In the eighties, food was something you coated in salad cream and stuffed your face with. These days it's taken on a holy veneer – it's all clean this and detox that. And the rules change by the day. You wake up to find that the food you always thought was OK now isn't. So it turns out sausages and olive oil give you cancer, rice is full of arsenic and smoothies are a one-way ticket to dentures. And as for all that apple juice and dried fruit you've been giving them – what were you *thinking*?

Taking your kids to McDonald's – a treat when you were growing up – has become something people don't admit to in polite society. Red meat is a no-no. (Or is it? You're never quite sure.) And don't even start on butter and milk. Your Gwyneth Paltrows and Ella Woodwards tell you to feed your kids kale crisps as a tasty treat (ha!), which only makes you feel worse when they live on oven chips and Mr Whippy from the van.

Even if you aren't the kind of parent who blends dates with raw cacao powder and tells them it's a brownie, you're likely to be affected by food neurosis. It's practically impossible not to be. So you find yourself poring over ingredients lists, wondering what xanthan gum is and whether or not it's bad. You ration their Easter eggs, forgetting that you used to stuff yours down in one sitting, and once ate so many you were sick all over your Cabbage Patch Kid.

You fret that they eat too much or too little, that they aren't getting enough protein or cruciferous vegetables, overlooking the fact that you yourself survived a whole decade living on cheese, chips and biscuit Boost bars. Christ, you grew up in an era when everything from pudding to potatoes came powdered in a packet. Maybe that's why you're so neurotic now.

Believing everything you read on forums

Back in the olden days, when women married at twenty-one and scrubbing the doorstep was something to do, new mothers had a coterie of sisters and aunties they could turn to for tips. Now, though, when we need advice, we tend not to turn to relatives so much. Because why would you, when you can consult a bunch of random strangers instead?

These days, if we've got a question – anything from 'When will I stop feeling low?' to 'Why has my baby got a flat head?' – we head straight for the internet. Because that way you get not just one opinion, but a dozen. It's fast, it's efficient, and it won't get drunk and tell everyone about your baby's freaky head.

The main problem with forums is that you're never sure who it is you're talking to. Posters are anonymous. You know nothing about them other than what you can judge from their usernames: Madcatlady (annoying), SW12tootsy (posh), TerryWogansCock (disturbing). So it's hard to tell how much credence you should give their opinions. Some people helpfully mark themselves out as idiots by sharing beliefs Josef Mengele would consider a bit off, but just as many loons wear the mask of the normal person. Without meeting them, you'd never know.

Read a bit further and you often come to realize these are people you wouldn't trust to give you directions to the park, let alone advice on vital health matters. Yet here you are, eagerly seeking their take on the very same subjects people study for years at medical school.

But going to the GP is a palaver. To even get an appointment, you have to go through an elaborate process of either turning up at the surgery first thing or phoning repeatedly at 8 a.m. until you're lucky enough to get through. It's easier to get Glastonbury tickets. Then you take time out of an already busy day to join a room full of elderly sick people, who sit there, depressing you, like the ghosts of Christmas future. No wonder you'd rather consult a crowd of strangers online.

And strangers online often say what you want to hear. If your child wakes up with weeping black pustules on her face, you want to hear from somebody whose child had the exact same thing and is now fine. Or you at least want to hear about whatever crazy juju they used to fix it when the GP had nothing to offer.

Unlike going to the doctor's, forums are entertaining and even mildly addictive, especially when people start bickering (which never takes long). They're a useful way of gauging how the world really thinks, as women vent opinions they'd be too scared to reveal to their NCT crowd. Forums are a place where people feel safe to let out their inner prick. Anonymity allows them to brag about the things they can't brag about to their friends, like the price of their engagement ring, or slag off people they can't usually slag off, like the other parents at their kids' school. It means they can give the juice on their embarrassing conditions and tell you the details of their disastrous sex lives.

And the topics covered are so wide-ranging. From the age limit on wearing a bikini, to what to do when you find your husband on a dating site, you can guarantee that someone, somewhere, is on a forum having a rant about it. It's testament to the addictive nature of these things that everybody on there seems to know each other. Just how much time is everybody spending on forums, you wonder?

It's fine if you take whatever you read with a handful of salt. But what you read tends to merge with what you've gleaned from newspapers and parenting books to form one big information soup in your head. You may find yourself dipping into this at random and regurgitating what you find as fact, saying with authority, 'I read somewhere that . . .', the implication being that you got it from a trusted, reliable source, not some bullshit online forum populated by halfwits and sociopaths.

People on forums might talk a lot of rubbish, but at least they talk it about a vast range of stuff – from where to eat in Cardiff, to whether it's normal for your husband to expect anal sex because he took you to Centre Parcs. And, let's face it, that's a fat lot more than your GP can do.

Being angry all the time

Along with brain fog and memory loss, one of the side effects of being so dog-tired and/or premenstrual all the time is a kind of constant, low-level rage. Whereas once your moods were as varied as the weather, these days your emotions run the gamut from angry to ballistic. For a surprisingly large part of the time you can find yourself feeling quietly furious, and longing to take it out on someone.

Whereas old you might have shied away from confrontation, and perhaps liked to think of yourself as a placid, easy-going sort of a person, these days you're like an eighties casual at an Old Firm match, constantly looking for a fight. *Just start on me*, you silently dare the woman behind you in the post office, who's glaring at you for addressing envelopes while keeping your place in the queue. *Go on, inspector, try throwing me off the train because I seem to have mislaid my ticket*. You may go so far as to find yourself imagining these exchanges in your head, plotting cutting retorts in the event that someone is naive enough to challenge you. But, frustratingly, they never do.

In much the same way, you're almost disappointed by how cool people are when you breastfeed in public. The media has led you to believe this is something close to sedition, liable to have you scolded by outraged geriatrics. You find yourself waiting for some ignorant cafe owner or security guard to admonish you, so that you can let rip about your right to *feed your baby*, and then make an enormous fuss about it afterwards on social media. Because how gratifying it must be to get to be that angry and indignant, yet so patently in the right. So it's annoying when nobody gives you a second glance, even when you make a hash of putting your boob away and it's nips out to the world.

Likewise, when your toddler throws a full-blown, buggy-breaking tantrum in the airport departure lounge, you're quietly willing someone to make a snide remark as you're in just the mood for telling them where to stick it. But instead your fellow passengers are annoyingly compassionate. The flight attendant brings you a bag of gummy bears and lets you board first. Another mother touches your arm and says, 'I feel your pain,' bringing you to tears with her kindness.

Those old ladies people promised you – the ones who tut and tell you that what your child needs is a good slap – don't seem to materialize, except for when you're at the supermarket and accidentally ram your trolley into one of them because it's loaded with children and you can't control it. But that's sort of your fault. At any rate, you're not going to get away with posting evil comments about them on Twitter.

All this means that there is no outlet for your anger. So instead you're left getting disproportionately annoyed with friends if they're late, or sending your partner texts full of CAPS LOCK SWEARING with no kisses at the end. Really, it's your partner who bears the brunt of all this. Every non-event is escalated in your head to become an example of how crap he is, and how badly he treats you, to the point that, if he so much as forgets to make the bed, it's just another example of how he doesn't need a wife, but a maid. And was that the role you signed up for? No it effing wasn't. SCREW YOU. And so on.

In fact, if you look through your text history with him, it's sort of embarrassing. It seems to mostly consist of fifty-word 'and another thing' missives. Along with the kind of abuse that, if he'd given it to you, would have had you dialling a solicitor. Sometimes you walk into a room and he's giving you that look, the one that says, 'Are you going to say sorry?' But, thanks to the memory loss, you can't even remember what it was you said.

Tiredness and PMT aside, you're not quite sure why you're so quick to anger these days. Although it doesn't help that everybody seems to be sabotaging you, with their messiness and their irritating habits and their refusal to rinse anything before they put it in the dishwasher, even though you've told them 50,000 times that it won't come out clean if they don't.

In fact, you have a horrible feeling that you may be turning into a nag. But that's a term you resent, too. Because the fact is, you wouldn't have to be a nag if people only did what you said the first time. What do they think, that you *want* to tell them sixteen times to put their pants in the laundry bin? Why can't they just do it without being asked? Gah.

These days your fuse isn't so much short as entirely absent. Other people, it transpires, are endlessly infuriating. But though you're more than happy dishing it out, you can find that you're not so good at taking it. If anyone *does* tell you off, or give you a dirty look, you're so shocked and unprepared for it you don't know how to react. Your brain is too slow to think of an off-the-cuff comeback. And you're so sensitive you take every piece of advice as a criticism, every comment as a judgement. It may be that you're not quite the breezy, carefree girl you once were. You're becoming one of those old ladies people warned you about.

Crying on the phone to BT

Dealing with call centres, or customer services, or taking things back to the shop – these were never exactly up there with your top-ten things to do. But such jobs only get harder when you become a mother. For a start, you're at home more, which tends to mean they fall to you. It's the maternity-leave swizz – you're not working, except that what you're doing is almost exactly like work, only without the pay cheque and the colleagues to flirt with.

So when your internet dies, or a direct debit mysteriously bounces, it's you who ends up getting on the phone to the bank or BT. Which is a bugger, as you're exhausted and frustrated enough without spending half an hour on hold listening to Mozart's Symphony No. 40. By the time you get past the call menu and through to a real live person, you can feel yourself teetering on the verge, your voice going all clipped and high-pitched, like when you were in trouble at school and trying not to cry in front of everybody.

You may try to claw back the upper hand by being as rude as you possibly can, peppering your complaint with sighs and tuts. In a bid to fake some gravitas, you may find yourself adopting the persona of 'outraged baroness', behaving as though this is the worst/most unhelpful call of this kind you've ever had, even though they all tend to follow pretty much the same pattern. If you're the super-confident type, you may even ask to speak to their supervisor. But it doesn't pay to forget that, ultimately, the call-centre operative holds the power, which they remind you of by hanging up so that you have to go through the whole bastard process all over again.

It seems as if calls like this are designed purely to frustrate you. You lose their passwords and fail their security checks. You forget to download their apps, so that every time you want to use their stupid service it becomes a protracted process, with you having to remember which bloody card you registered with them in the first place.

The whole experience is especially draining if you're calling about something you lack the vocabulary to discuss, like a tech issue. Then it's sod's law that it's a man on the end of the line, who proceeds to patronize you to death, breaking his instructions down to idiot level and leaving long pauses before answering your questions, just so there can be no doubt that he thinks you're a moron. You may find yourself going in circles for a while, before it dawns on you both that you are getting nowhere.

'Have you checked that it's plugged in?' he asks in desperation. *Aargh*, you think, *I hate you, horrible, condescending man.* 'Yes, of course,' you say, before remembering that you have done no such thing. Your embarrassment makes you even more annoyed. How can you possibly make this his fault? In the end you don't know who to be angrier with – him, for his dumb, sexist views, or yourself, for reinforcing them all.

And while you appreciate that, yes, his job is a challenging and thankless one, and that, yes, you may perhaps come across as a huffy, self-righteous twat, still he and the other call-centre operatives make no allowances for your fragile mental state and show no humanity, refusing to stray from the script and show you a little compassion.

It's the perfect storm: the hormonal woman and the deliberately belligerent telephone operative, thrown together in the ring. You may understand this is a fight you're unlikely to win and try to level with them, wailing, 'I've been up all night!' – a statement that, if you're not careful, will be taken the wrong way.

This is bad enough on the phone, but in a shop it's plain humiliating. Here you are, a woman in your fourth decade, welling up because the man in the Apple Store doesn't believe your story about a manufacturing fault and won't give you a new keyboard for free. Doesn't he even know how tired you are? It's all you can do not to stamp your foot and cry.

And you find yourself crying in all sorts of inappropriate places. In the park. At the GP's. At the Ryanair customer-services desk when they charge you NINETY QUID because you forgot to check in online before you flew. There are times you don't bother wearing mascara because you don't quite trust yourself. Because emotionally you aren't yet capable of a fraught encounter with a stranger. Or not of emerging from one with your dignity intact, at least.

Becoming a hypochondriac

If the world has made a sport of baiting women with fear and anxiety about their health, then the ultimate gladiators must be pregnant woman and her comrade, new mother.

There are whole industries devoted to making pre- and post-natal women feel terrified about all the hideous things that can happen to them before, during and after birth. The expectant woman learns early on that if she hasn't already got AIDS, and can manage to avoid miscarriage, pre-eclampsia and death during childbirth, she can still look forward to plenty of other illnesses. Flesh-eating bacteria, mastitis, Lyme disease, post-partum psychosis and a whole load of other shit from hell can scupper what is supposed to be the happiest time of a woman's life (nothing quite beats that afternoon on the terrace at Space in Ibiza, mind).

As we trundle through the scans, checks and blood tests that punctuate pregnancy and the first year after birth, it can feel as though some medical professionals only exist to put the willies up us. Who knows if these charlatans are really qualified in anything? In those early days you are so tired and vulnerable, they could turn up at your house and point the remote control at your baby and you wouldn't question it.

They are really just good people going about their jobs, but all the well-meaning scaremongering does often seem to leave a scar. Because once the chrysalis hatches and you become a fully-fledged mother, you realize you are officially a hypochondriac.

Yes, you, who as a student survived on lager and Scotch eggs from the service station. You, whose hands are scarred with the drunken burns you got back when fags didn't come with an on-switch. You, who rode helmetless on the back of a moped through the Goan jungle with a fireman from Glasgow, gurning your face off on God-knows-what and singing that song about doing it like mammals on the Discovery Channel at the top of your lungs. SIGH.

Yes, we're sorry to announce that *that* you got flushed away with the placenta (unless you buried it or ate it, in which case things are worse than we thought). It was replaced by this new you – the one who frets about every teensy-tiny aspect of your health and your child's. The you who regularly self-diagnoses catastrophic, statistically impossible conditions that signify the imminent end of your life.

It begins with the late-night hospital runs. Conscientiously doing your research into every possible cause of infant death, you memorize the meningitis checklist early on (boy, that's a great leaflet). You have plenty of time to do this as you stop sleeping, so that you can make sure the baby is breathing throughout the night. You become a regular at your local A&E, racing there every time the baby has a temperature and cries when you shine a massive torch in his face (the leaflet says they don't like bright lights!).

Then, spurred on by the glorious internet with all its ghoulish information and shocking images, you move through an arc of rare tropical diseases and Victorian-sounding conditions. You diagnose your son with rickets (because his legs look a bit bendy) and wonder out loud if your daughter has extra joints (because her little chubby arms just don't look right). Every time your child misbehaves you label him with whichever syndrome you were reading about in the doctors' waiting room. These are disorders that the health professionals just can't seem to recognize, despite their training and experience, and your persistent visits to the surgery.

Having exhausted the possibilities, you are forced to accept that your child is in fact healthy. So now, hallucinatory due to a full nine months without any significant shut-eye, you turn on yourself, diagnosing conditions that include, but are not limited to:

- **cirrhosis**, because you have white spots on your fingernails and did drink quite a lot of wine in your twenties.
- **early menopause**, because of all the hair in the plughole and because you are so tearful all the time.
- **lupus**, because you have an ulcer and do look a bit like a wolf, or at least a dog with those jowls – look at them! – and have a bit of a headache.
- **dementia**, because you forget why you are going up the stairs when you are halfway up them.
- **osteoporosis**, because everything hurts.

Then one day the baby sleeps through until 7 a.m., and you wake up and feel like a superhero. And you realize the only thing that was wrong with you was chronic fatigue. You still look a bit like a dog though.

Noticing that your friends got richer than you

Now that you think about it, it was never a level playing field. Even at university, when everybody was so skint they kept the heating off and bought Kwik Save No Frills teabags, there were always some people who could afford to live the high life: the ones who took trains rather than coaches, and smoked Marlboro Lights instead of Superkings.

It wasn't a big deal though. Nor was it after university, when you were all in crap-paying first jobs. As long as you had enough money for the next round, you were OK. You could eat in nice restaurants and have the odd splurge in Urban Outfitters, because if God hadn't meant for you to do that, he wouldn't have invented overdrafts, would he? And there were credit cards! Which people were willing to give to you! And they wouldn't do that if they thought you couldn't afford to pay them back, right?

So even though on paper your income in no way covered the lifestyle you were living, you and your friends were, again, pretty much on a level. You all rented flats of varying degrees of shitness. You all took the night bus. You were like the girls in *Girls*, if they lived in Zone 3 and ate a lot of chicken shish kebabs. Sure, there were differences between you: some of your friends had fancier clothes than you did, and travelled to more far-flung places, but those were superficial things. I mean, who cared about that, really?

But then you grow up and have children, and suddenly the gap between your incomes becomes glaringly apparent. And it isn't about clothes or handbags or who has a nicer sofa, but who can afford a cleaner or a nanny, or someone to do the ironing – someone to take away the drudgery, in other words. Even with such luxuries, you hear these friends complain about how tough it is and a small part of you can't help but think, 'Sod *off* – you don't know how easy you've got it.'

Because these are the fortunate women for whom life,

post-children, continues pretty much as before. They can still go out in the evening, get their hair cut or do a spinning class. They have someone to take over in the morning, which means they can stay out late and grab the odd lie-in. They're the ones who can afford to actually go away, instead of spending hours researching holidays online, only to tot up the price for all of you and promptly can the idea.

It's tougher still for those in London, where mentalist house prices force all but the lucky few into poky flats. This is fine when you're too young and drunk to notice, but wears thin when you're a family of four squeezed into the two-bed you imagined you'd move out of years ago. Meanwhile, people in your circle are buying actual houses, with gardens and guest bathrooms and space for an au pair. And as you talk to them about their planned loft conversion and fabulous new garden office, you try not to tear your eyes out with the wretched unfairness of it all.

And you're forced to confront the fact that you have made terrible life choices. Because it turns out that the friends with the demanding corporate jobs you were once so sneery about are the ones who had it sussed. Back in the day you'd look at them, with their officewear and their spreadsheets, and sigh, 'I just couldn't do that.' But now you know that in fact you very much could do that, and wish to God you had.

More irritating still are the ones who marry rich – this really is a kick in the teeth. You console yourself by imagining how miserable and unfulfilled they are, but sadly you know this just isn't true. The only real comfort comes from bitching about them with other, equally poor friends. 'I wouldn't know what to do with myself all day,' you lie, even though you can think of a thousand things you'd do, all of which are way more fun than whatever it is you're up to right now. You snipe about their extensions and how they've ruined the character of the house, like someone died and made you the head of English Heritage.

Everybody knows that envy is an ugly emotion, which is why most of us try to keep a check on it. So this is the time to remind yourself of those friends who've got it as hard, if not tougher, than you do. It's human nature to look up rather than down, so this doesn't always come naturally. But you try to remind yourself how lucky you are, and hope you'll be granted the serenity to be pleased for your friends' good fortune, and the wisdom to know it doesn't matter. And that their garden office leaks.

Losing the plot over Christmas

Christmas changes so much when you have children. You go through a funny phase in your twenties where it all gets a bit *Groundhog Day* – where you go home and get trashed in your old haunts, before doing midnight mass in an ironic way and stumbling home at an ungodly hour. On the day itself, you sleep in late, because – let's face it – lunch with ageing relatives isn't a prospect you feel like leaping out of bed for. You've asked for a cheque so you've got nothing to open, the telly's crap, no one buys you selection boxes any more and . . . bah, humbug.

So it's a relief, then, when kids come along and Christmas takes on a new significance. Admittedly this means coming to terms with your loss of status. Now you're lucky if you get a paperback and a scented candle, while your tight-arsed parents even have the nerve to break it to you that you're probably too old for a stocking. Your kids, meanwhile, get to work their way through a stash Elton John would consider excessive.

But, though you lose out on the present front, there is a subtle power shift. For what may be the first time, you host Christmas at your house, rather than spending it at your parents' or in-laws'. This means that, for once, you are Christmas Boss-Lady. Which means that, finally, you can address your niggles about previous Christmases, and the overriding sense you had that everybody was doing it all wrong.

Because, let's be honest, the Christmases of your childhood were a little basic. Where were the Yule logs and pigs-in-blankets? The smoked-salmon starters and the stollen? It wasn't Sunday-supplement Christmas at all, but 1980s Christmas, with an over-reliance on bread sauce and Josceline Dimbleby's Sainsbury's cookbooks. Your Christmas, by contrast, is going to be the perfect mixture of traditional and modern, of jolly and chic. It will be an amalgamation of the adverts, magazine spreads and films that have seeped into your psyche over the decades. Nothing less than Martha Stewart-league festivities will do.

A voice in your head may try and tell you that you are setting yourself up for a fall, and that striving for perfection is doomed to end in failure. But another, bossier voice is enjoying being Controller of Christmas, who decides what time everybody eats and whether you're going to watch a movie, go for a walk or play a board game. You decide to create your own family traditions, such as buying a fancy bauble for the tree every year, and making sure everybody has new pyjamas on Christmas Eve.

You wonder which chef to throw your weight behind (you may prefer Nigel, but when it comes to Christmas, Nigella has it in the bag). You buy her book and set yourself the task of making three-quarters of it. You even give serious thought to whether you're supposed to brine your turkey or coat it in butter-soaked muslin cloths.

But it turns out that the quest for the perfect Christmas is a little like the quest for a perfect wedding. You can become Yule-zilla, who sulks because you bought the tree too early and now, not even three weeks into December, it's looking hunched and dehydrated. You spend half your life on your knees with a handheld vac, hoovering up needles and shards of bauble as, between them, the toddler and the dog are on a mission to smash them all. You bark at your partner, who doesn't seem to be pulling his weight, and isn't getting nearly as het up as you are about the fact that the turkey has to be ordered in advance and Heston's whatever-it-is may sell out.

When it comes to gifts, you have the genius idea that, instead of being suckered into buying people more expensive trash they don't need, you will make brownies or truffles and present them in something stylishly functional, like Kilner jars or brown paper. Three days before Christmas you realize that you could live twelve lifetimes and still never be the woman who makes her own truffles. This late epiphany means you miss the Amazon deadline and have to face the actual shops, with no ideas or childcare. In desperation, you decide you're going to theme this year's presents – i.e. buy everybody the same thing.

On your return, you get to spend two solid days cooking and have a minor breakdown because no one sells those lady's finger biscuit things for the trifle. Then you remember – shit, the presents! So, instead of drinking fizz and holding court at 11 p.m. on Christmas Eve, you are up to your eyeballs in scissors and Sellotape. You realize that Malcolm Gladwell's whole 10,000-hours theory is bollocks, because after thirty years of practice, you're still no better at wrapping presents than you ever were.

On the day itself, your Christmas does not look as idyllic as the one you had in your head. Instead, it looks like a shitload of clearing up that no one's going to help you with as they're too busy enjoying being let off the hook. More annoyingly still, you are not sensing nearly enough gratitude. No one seems overwhelmed with appreciation for the mince pies and tree cookies, which admittedly you don't much fancy eating either. You have the feeling they'd have been as happy with shop-bought ones – perhaps happier, as it turns out baking isn't a gift you were blessed with.

And what's that? People are interfering with your carefully laid plans, turning on *EastEnders* and staring at the floor when you suggest a nice walk. The walk is non-negotiable – you've already planned the photos in your head. You've got the route mapped out and everything. You gently coax – for which read 'bully' – them into it.

The walk gives you the chance to muse on the expense of it all. Even though you forgot about the clove-studded ham and the gingerbread house, and baulked at the price of the stair garland, you could still probably have covered lunch at the Wolseley for what you've spent. It's all you can do not to go around telling everybody how much it all was. 'Enjoyed that Manchego, did you? Fifteen pounds. No, you don't get very much for that, do you? And do you know how much turkeys are? No, I didn't either . . .'

But this quest for a picture-perfect Christmas isn't just you being mad. As a mother, it is your job to create Christmas, and a lifetime of propaganda means you feel you owe it to your kids to make it magical. But what with the shows and the German markets, the outdoor ice-skating and the trips to see Santa, the Christmas industry is already out of hand. Suddenly you understand why your mum just whammed a turkey in the oven, cracked open the Liebfraumilch and let everyone get on with watching *Indiana Jones and the Temple of Doom*. It's not just her, either. Later you read that Nigella gets caterers at Christmas, the treacherous cow.

Thinking soft-play centres are the best invention ever

Kids today have got it made. Now, even the most bog-standard playground gives them the full Costa Rican rainforest experience, with zip lines and rope bridges. There are indoor theme parks where kids can spend the day role-playing in a child-sized city. They have children's cafes and family festivals. It's not like it was in your day, when there was literally nothing to do.

OK, so maybe you had the odd bowling trip. And there was the leisure centre, of course, and the ice rink, with its

Hammond-organ muzak and pervading smell of burnt fat and vinegar. But mostly you were outdoors in all weathers in someone's garden or a park that thought it was a big deal if it had an old tyre on a rope for a swing.

You don't remember there being much in the way of soft play, either. Certainly you see why kids love it. They get to hare around as they please, hurling themselves from slides and bouncing off the walls. There's a part of you that always wants to have a go yourself. But – besides being a rainy-day activity that isn't the library – soft play serves a valuable purpose for you too.

Because if you don't already know what kind of mother you are, one visit to a soft-play centre will tell you. Perhaps you're the type who sees it as a respite – the chance to grab a coffee and sit indoors while the kids wreck somewhere that isn't your house. It gives you the opportunity to catch up with your mates and mess about on your phone. Mothers in this camp tend to take a hands-off approach, believing that kids should be allowed to get on with it, and that as long as they're not beating each other up, it's kind of fine. You might say that mothers in this camp are natural-born slackers.

Or perhaps you wouldn't dream of being so laissez-faire and simply leaving your kids to it. Instead you're at their side, helping them over obstacles and cheerleading as they climb the scramble net. Is this you? If so, you're probably a closet helicopter mother.

Soft play can be a struggle for helicopter mother, who resents slack mother for taking it easy when she's working so hard at being enthusiastic and engaged, and making sure her child doesn't bite someone or wee in the ball pit.

Slack mother, meanwhile, tends to think that helicopter mother is bizarre and should grow up and get off the play-frame.

Never will you see two parenting philosophies collide more starkly than at a soft-play centre. Look hard enough and you'll often spot both sides glaring at each other, attaching themselves to those they see as like-minded souls. Helicopter mother longs for slack mother's off-spring to step out of line so that she has an excuse to pull her up about it. Often this doesn't happen and she's forced to settle for tutting and looking huffy. But sometimes these encounters end in words – or an angry visit to an internet forum.

Online, there are no end of threads filled with mothers raging about the other children at soft play. Often there's an undercurrent of snobbery. 'She must have been play-ing truant,' someone types furiously of the older child who pushed her toddler. If a mother wants everyone to know the type of child she was dealing with, she'll write something like, 'He was drinking a Fruit Shoot.'

It's not nice, but as mothers we are so used to being judged, if someone gives us the chance to look down on another parent, we're all over it. And soft play, being crowded and all welcoming, is not short on opportunities. Complaints about other parents are rife: 'They never look up from their phones!' aggrieved women hammer into key-boards. Or, 'They bring their children who are full of cold!' Other mothers respond offering support and their own tales of soft-play hell. Either that or they use it as a chance to congratulate themselves ('I'd never let my child behave like that'; 'I *always* take hand sanitizer and Dettol wipes').

All this really shows is just how cushy things have become. It's not so long ago that children were playing on abandoned bomb sites. Now they're playing on giant cushions, with paid staff supervising their every move – and still parents fret about germs or whether some kid blocked theirs on the slide.

It's a shame, because if we could all get over ourselves, we'd see that soft play really is a winner for everybody. After all, when the kids eventually come off, sweating and happy, you can reassure yourself that they've been engaging in physical exercise and must have burned a thousand calories. In other words, you've done your duty, so it's fine if they go home and watch three hours of *Peppa Pig*.

Once you understand this, and accept that it's OK for parents to sit on the sidelines (after all, if every mother got in the ball pit, there wouldn't be much room for the kids), you start to think that soft play is kind of brilliant. You start wondering if you shouldn't go there every rainy day. You look into getting membership and think how great it would be to have their party there. After all, it would totally take away the stress. Instead of stuffing party bags, you could sit in the cafe, chatting with your mates and messing about on your phone. And what's so bad about that?

On the Act

Not having sex with your husband

You're not sure why you don't want to have sex with him any more. You sometimes wonder if you're simply acting out a script – becoming the joyless old battleaxe wife – because somewhere in your subconscious you think that's what you're supposed to do. Maybe if you hadn't watched all those episodes of *Last of the Summer Wine* as a child, where the married woman was Nora Batty and the sexy lady was a tart with big boobs called Marina, you might not have this strange sense that sex isn't for you any more.

Because you're still very fond of your husband, despite the relentless moaning about him you do, often to his face. And it's not like sex with him is such an awful thing to endure. You've been known to enjoy it, over the years. You used to have quite a lot of sex with him, actually. And it was good. You had it all worked out. You both knew which buzzers went off when. But somewhere along the line, you seemed to stop having it. And now you hardly ever do. What's more, you find yourself avoiding it. Washing your proverbial hair. Why should that be so?

After the baby is born it's a simple case of excruciating

pain. It hurts. You've stitches holding your Mary together, or your belly, or both. Wherever they are, no penis is going near the area formerly known as your vagina. When the midwife asks if you've thought about contraception, only a few short hours after you've passed a baby, you spit out your tea. Not having sex ever again, that's my contraception! You think this is a brilliant answer, along with every woman who's ever given birth and had their midwife ask this question.

Then it's a matter of the snuffling creature attached to your nipples. No one wants to have sex with a baby attached to their nipples. And your baby never seems to latch off. He's clamped on like his life depends on it. Which it does. Ever the gent, your husband makes his excuses and departs for the spare room, muttering about work and not wanting to be tired. Yeah, sleep well, chicken shit, you sob through your tears. He stays there for the next nine months, only returning when he can be absolutely certain the child has a bottle and is zipped into a Grobag, with no means of escape, in his own room.

Even once the night feeding has stopped and normal patterns emerge, it's rare to find yourselves in bed and awake at the same time, never mind in bed, awake and in the mood for sex. Although you do notice, from his ever-present hard-on, that he is definitely horny. He is perma-horny. You? Less so. You were up in the night/ have to get up in an hour/had no sleep/blah tired blah/ he was snoring/need sleep/so tired. You are tired, OK? And what kind of a crazed sex beast is he that he would make you shag him when you are so tired? He retreats to have 'a shower'. And you know what's happening in there, and feel a twinge of guilt. Which gives way to relief that it isn't happening anywhere near you, and you can go back to sleep.

It's not always like this. Occasionally, you have enough sleep – and therefore good will – in the bank to be vaguely interested. The kids are hooked into an episode of whatever-it-is downstairs, and you have exactly eleven minutes to go wild. And you have sex with your husband. You even want to as much as he does – in theory, at least. But it's hard to really get behind it – give yourself over to deep sexual abandon – when you can hear Mr Bloom giving it large about recycling, and have to keep stopping because you think that's someone crying/choking/coming upstairs. He seems less easily distracted than you, more able to concentrate on the task in hand. Honestly, it's as though you are wired differently. And you wonder if you can be arsed if it's going to always be like this. You have little enough time as it is. And some other uptight, frigid stuff about a book and a cup of tea.

Still, you're keen to heed the advice of Mariella and Pamela, and all the other ballsy-older-lady sex columnists, the ones who warn against the loss of physical relations and recommend wearing blindfolds and scheduling sex in on Tuesday afternoons to keep the spark alive. Either that or you can still hear your mum reminding you about doing 'your duty' not long after you had the baby. You assumed it was a joke, but realize now that this is no laughing matter.

So you book a weekend away. Tell yourself you need to make time for this, because it's so important. And you send the kids to Grandma's and pack the new book/sex toy/drugs that you're pinning your hopes on. And off you go to some overpriced, overdesigned boutique bolthole in the Cotswolds, where you're hoping to find your libido has checked in too.

But now, instead of the tiredness, it's the pressure to have a good time that stops you wanting to have one. You're a sort of warped sexual mule: you know you need to get out of this box you're in, but you're damned if anyone's going to force you out of it, Mr & Mrs Smith minibreak or no. Besides which, you're a bit fucked off, actually. You decide to let him know this around bottle of wine number two, having been distant and tight-lipped since you arrived.

Because it's always you who sorts everything out when you go away. He just packs his own stuff and walks out the door. He did nothing to help before you left. If it was down to him you'd never – and on and on and on you go, sabotaging the whole thing. Is it on purpose? You're not sure. By Sunday morning you feel like you might be able to loosen up, but it's home time now. And secretly you're glad, because you've got a lot of ironing to do before school tomorrow. And you think you can't be arsed if it's going to always be like this. You'd rather go away with your friends. At least then he could look after the kids and do the ironing.

And the tiredness and the busyness, the same-old familiarity and the seething resentment become the norm. And sex becomes something you can only find the good humour to do when you're drunk. Or hung-over. Either way, you often can't remember the details.

You feel bad about this. You feel bad for your husband, because you do love him and you know he wants to be having a lot more sex than he is. He'll probably have an affair if you don't start putting out. A small part of you wonders how much you'd mind, if it meant you didn't have to worry about it. And you feel bad for yourself, too. Because, the truth is, you do have sexual urges. You'd probably have sex with a handsome stranger against the wall if one happened to walk in right now, with a wall. But you can't seem to want to do it much with your own husband. The father of your children.

You talk to your friends and find out that quite a lot of them aren't having sex with their husbands, either. In fact, you discover, some of them haven't done it for years – consecutive ones. Others describe clinical routines involving tissues and the phrase 'finish yourself off'. Others say they are so bored by the predictability of it that they can't imagine doing it with their husband. Ever. Again.

And, between you, you decide that the way you feel is probably to do with science or evolution. Maybe you're not supposed to be having all this sex – aren't men supposed to be off spreading their seed? Maybe it's just a big media construct. Or perhaps it's because you've had children, and your energy and affection is spent on them. Whatever it is you decide on, you agree that the way you feel is normal and natural. And you feel much better, and decide to book a girls' weekend away to celebrate.

Being a bored housewife

The downside of not getting divorced is that it tends to mean you end up staying married. Sure, this has its benefits – there's something beautiful about being with the same person for decades, and you totally aspire to being one of those elderly couples you occasionally see walking hand-in-hand, the ones who've been together a lifetime. But the middle years, before you become that elderly testament to the power of commitment, can be kind of a drag.

Because the workload of parenthood takes the thrill out of even the best relationships. You witness it with your friends and you see it in your own life: the ongoing fight about who's got it harder, the passive aggression, the skill with which you manage to bring an undercurrent of screw-you to every exchange.

You watch other couples snap at each other about what their child does or doesn't need. 'I think you'll find she's hungry!' one barks, gloating like mad if the child then eats. You find yourself rowing over everything, from who empties the dishwasher more to whether or not your child likes banana. It's horrible to be around and it's horrible to be in. If you're still having sex after all that, then clearly you're the forgiving type.

Occasionally you find yourself wondering, is this it? Does it only go downhill from here? Surely I'm too young to be celibate. You envy the teenagers snogging at bus stops and groping each other up at the cinema, the thrill they get when the right person calls. You remember the days when you and your partner would send each other flirty texts. Now your texts fall into one of two categories: the demand (*can you just . . .?*) and the bollocking (*why don't you just . . .?*).

To get the spark back, you contemplate going retro wife – wearing foxy underwear, mixing Martinis and asking concerned questions about his day. But that sounds like a huge effort, and who drinks Martinis at home, anyway? Frankly, it's easier just to develop a crush on someone else.

But who to fancy? This needs to be someone safe – after all, you don't actually want to end your marriage. You read *Madame Bovary*. You're aware that situations like this don't tend to end well for women. Still, it would be nice to have someone buff to look at.

Colleagues are a bad idea, because that way danger lies. Same goes with random fit men in bars, although good luck meeting many of those. Handymen are useful because they come round to the house and you can fantasize about it all going a bit whoops-window-cleaner-where-are-my-knickers? But your handyman is not sexy. He wears skanky tracksuit bottoms and talks too much. He thinks the plural of mouse is mices.

When he comes, the plumber doesn't do much for you either. His name is Leroy and he's either boss-eyed or has a touch of Asperger's. In any case, he doesn't look at you, only the wall behind your head. He also arrives at a bad time, when the kitchen is cluttered with breakfast chaos and the bin smells of poo. It's not an atmosphere conducive to sexytime.

So you try and fancy the other dads. You are now on riskier turf, but hey, you are bored and need eye candy. However, the depressing truth is that the other dads aren't that fit. They are like older, fatter, greyer versions of the men you knew back in the day. Many have embraced the beard, a fashion that makes all men at least 20 per cent less hot. 'I don't look as wrecked as the other dads,' your husband says proudly, smearing Regaine into his bald patch. And he is right.

There is always one father who, by virtue of not being a complete minger, becomes sexy dad. Occasionally sexy dad makes everybody's day by coming to the playground. But it's hard, even for sexy dad, to be attractive in natural daylight, dishing out jam sandwiches and intervening in arguments about who called who a farter. Why is he in the playground on a weekday afternoon anyway, you wonder? And why are you judging him for that?

Other dads are really not a goer, you conclude. They are also married to your friends. So you end up perving over men clearly too young for you – the barista in your local coffee shop, the guy in the artisan bakery – who are just the right mixture of attractive and non-marriage-threatening. Not that they notice you, the drawn-looking woman yelling at her kids to stop touching the cakes.

Hot barista asks your name when you order coffee, even though you've ordered it from him thirty times before. And it comes as a blow to learn that you are not the woman young men fancy any more. To be that woman, you'd have to go down the route of fillers and manicures, and spending every other Saturday in the hairdressers. And even then, let's face it, you'd be a novelty shag. So, for you, life is easier if you stick to what you know. Which is how you come to appreciate the secret to a long-lasting marriage . . .

Fancying younger men

You never really understood why they called it *Desperate Housewives*. Desperate for what? Now you know. Desperate for hot sex against a tree with a ripped young gardener, that's what. Desperate for a fumble in an alleyway with a sexy student. Desperate for steamy windows in the back of the car with the neighbour's lodger. Desperate for plain and simple sexual badness with a younger man, basically. You don't know how or why it happened, but it has crept up on you, this undeniable lady-lust for the newer model.

Suddenly you see them wherever you go. They come round to fix the dodgy light in the kitchen and to trim the hedges. They serve you lunch at the cafe. They are in the field, standing there like James Dean, while you walk the dog. You fancied your nephew's nice friend from university recently. And your husband's younger cousin. You didn't use to notice this generation so much. Now they're everywhere. And they're hot. When did they get so hot? Men your age when you were that age were never this hot. They were all kebab-fat and nicotine fingernails. They had smelly hair and wore the same clothes every day and made jokes about Gary Glitter because it rhymed with shitter. This new breed looks good. Really good. They're charming, stylish, they have proper haircuts in proper styles. They're clean. You sound like your grandmother.

And you can't help thinking how easy it would be. You've seen *The Graduate*. You know what MILF means. All men want a fuck, right? Just a note passed discreetly as you pass in the bar, or a text message with instructions: *My house, 10 a.m., Tuesday. I'll be waiting for you in the bedroom.*

It's not just you either. It's happening to all the women you know. Now, on those interminable Girls' Nights Out, when groups of young men enter the room, you get all silly and start quoting those two fat old women from

Harry Enfield and Chums. 'Young man!' you all shriek, just loud enough so they can hear you. You may even get chatting to one and ask him to guess how old you are. You let yourself feel chuffed when he lies and tells you you look younger than you are, even though he knows how old you are really, because you're friends with his mum.

And there it is. Mum. You're a mum. A MILF maybe on a good day, with plenty of make-up and soft lighting, but MILF starts with Mum. And even if you managed to get the younger man in the sack, you'd still have the stretch marks and the saggy post-breastfeeding boobs to prove it. You wouldn't be Mrs Robinson, all ballsy and in control. You'd be Mrs You, all worried about the state of your bikini line and whether the neighbours could hear. And suddenly the familiar comfort of the older man – maybe even the one you had the kids with – feels like the only thing you are desperate for.

Sex and the single mum

Not all parental partnerships weather the shit-storm that is young children. Statistically, almost half of the UK's marriages end in divorce. Who knows what the figures are for those sensible enough not to spend a year's earnings on a tent full of bunting and a new frock? But let's say it's lots. Is this a depressing thought? Or is it kind of groovy? Are we all eventually going to live in communes, guys? Who knows? One thing's for sure, if your relationship ends, and you ever feel game enough to try again, you're going to have to think about doing it – having S.E.X. –

with someone else. Here are some things to consider when getting back on the horse:

Getting used to a new wang

If you've been making sweet love to the same man for many years, you are probably so accustomed to the size and form of his appendage that your vaginal walls have taken on its shape in relief. A bit like one of those mouldable gel mouthguards your son has for rugby. You have become so familiar with your ex slipping it in from behind while you're trying to get five more minutes sleep that you know every ripple and vein, literally with your eyes closed. So a new guy's schlong is a slippery thing to get to grips with. Be it longer or shorter, thinner or fatter, it may take a while to get the square peg in the round hole. It may hit new places, and miss others. It might be a different colour, or wear its hat at a jaunty new angle. It might feel like a whole new ball game. But remember when you thought you couldn't work out Twitter? And your new spiralizer? It's all about practice. You have to start using it, and see what happens.

Being ready for action
(see also: Waxing and the single mum, p. 77)

No more getting milk from the garage in your pyjamas and a coat. No more going to spinning class in a man's T-shirt and those saggy leggings from Tesco. No more eating anything with garlic or spinach in before going out. No more drinking red wine all night and looking like a hag. No letting your roots grow, or your moustache, or your eyebrows. No between-waxes hair of any description. No more big knickers with the period stains. No more grey bras. No more dropping the ball for a second. Because any man in any petrol station, at any exercise class, in any supermarket queue, could be the new one. And any night could be sex night.

Having sex in a strange place

If you were having the sexuals during Saturday-morning *Milkshake* for most of your married life, the chances are you came to favour a small number of regular locations for your lovemaking. These may have included under the duvet, on top of the duvet and occasionally locked in the bathroom.

Sometimes you may even have done it in the lounge – racy – when you got back drunk from a dinner party and felt briefly grateful for the man you had, and not the one you had to sit next to.

While wholly unexciting, these places were at least familiar to you. You knew where the exits were, your best angle in the mirror; that you could walk out of your bedroom backwards and get to the toilet in one quick leap, all without having to get dressed.

So when you start a new relationship it can be terrifying to find yourself exposed – not only emotionally, but physically too. At a hotel? You're probably so drunk you can't remember where the en suite is, for starters. Worse than that, there are all these unfamiliar lights to contend with, and those mirrors giving him unauthorized views of your derrière.

At his house? No chance of reaching for your dressing gown when you want to freshen up, love. You have to go full-on, brazen naked to his bathroom, possibly even with the lights on. The other option is to put your pants and whatever else back on under the duvet. This not only gets all the associated sex fluids on your nice new pants, but also tells him you lack body confidence – which is the one thing men really find sexy, right? We know this because magazines with unrealistic, airbrushed women on the front tell us so. Plus his furniture makes different noises and everything is at different heights. Getting jiggy in his bedroom is like being on the sex-edit of *The Crystal Maze*.

If you can't go home because your mum is babysitting and you can't go to his, perhaps because he lives with his mum, you may find yourself parked up in a lay-by reliving the sex of your teenage years. Only now you're both old, and much too big for the front seat, and when he tries to mount you it all gets a bit much and he spunks all over your dry-clean-only silk dress.

Talking a new language

A few set words and phrases to provide encouragement and support are common between established lovers. You may favour a filthy approach, all 'pull my hair' and 'spank me'. Or perhaps your style is more nurturing – 'Oh, yes, fill me up, big boy,' and not much can beat a simple: 'I love your massive cock.' Whatever language you've been speaking all these years, it's not going to make any sense to your new, essentially foreign, boyfriend. Together you'll need to forge a new dialect. It will be embarrassing and you may make mistakes at first, especially if you're a chatterbox and he's a deaf mute. But you'll soon find you can get by in hotels and on public transport.

Getting used to new 'habits'

Sharing the sensual feast with a spouse or long-term partner means you get to know which flavours and courses you both like best. You fall into reassuringly familiar habits, ordering the same dishes from the menu whenever you eat out. You know they might want to skip the starters and go straight to mains. They know you need to work up an appetite if you're going to digest things successfully. And so on.

The new sex you're having is likely to be with someone also coming from a long-term relationship, or just someone old, as may unfortunately be the case now that you are also old. (NB This theory doesn't really stand up for cougars, who are essentially fucking the hot waiters, the lucky bitches.) So you're going to have to try some different dishes on the menu. Turns out not everyone likes the same thing as you or your ex. You are going to have to try some new flavours.

Mostly, this is a rewarding experience for everyone. Who knew about that position where you're face down and he lies on top of you – but *facing the other way*! How does he even get in there? Better hope your feet don't smell, though his do a bit. And did you wax your toes? Anyway, it's amazing what you discover when you go à la carte.

Occasionally, though, you may find yourself saddled with a massive plate of something you can't stomach. When he suggests a trip to the local graveyard – just you, him and his collection of paddles – you may be forced to admit that you're not really keen on this fusion food, and have ordered unwisely. Make a mental note never to come here again.

Waxing and the single mum

There's been a paradigm shift in the way we wax since you last had sex with someone who wasn't your husband. Back in the day, you might have had a bikini wax before your holidays, and kept things tidy with a nail-scissors trim and a tube of Immac (back when it was called Immac).

During the childbearing years, everything may have gone a little wild down there. But were you even bothered? It's not like anyone but him was going to see it. And he'd seen it with a blood-soaked head coming out of it, so frankly he could deal with a few stragglers. You'd heard this stuff about vajazzling and Hollywood waxes, you knew the feminists were up in arms about anal bleaching, but it all seemed kind of irrelevant to you, who only ever had quick sex under the duvet before getting up to make the kids eggy bread.

But now your privates are on parade again, lady. And while your inner feminist knows that all this hair removal is at best just do-it-yourself porn, at worst infantilism, you can't help fretting about the way your Mary looks these days. A major part of you wants to rock a seventies vibe and not give a shit about your hairy muff – since that's what's supposed to be there and not an earring or a neon landing strip. Still, a small but persistently nagging part of you worries that you are not going to live up to the expectations of modern man. Should you ever find yourself in a situation where he is close enough to perform an inspection, that is.

And yes, you know you shouldn't want to be with the guy who can't forgive a little bush, but think too far along the it's-only-natural track, and you might as well never wear make-up or brush your hair, right? And so you venture forth to the waxing table and put yourself through the humiliation of having it torn out by a girl young enough to be your daughter, who you get the feeling has seen more fannies than your midwife, and talks to you about lips and clits as if she was getting a round in.

And whether you go full Hollywood or just 'extend' your regular wax, whether you get 'round the back' or keep it strictly window-shopping, whether you love your new nunny or feel kind of freaky – whatever the outcome, you're trapped. Because now you have to keep going back to have it done again every few weeks, in case you get that surprise inspection. Unless, that is, you don't mind looking like the last chicken in Sainsbury's when you get down to monkey business with that new man.

So while you might get to have all the fun and passion that goes with a new fling, you can't help feeling envious of your happily married friends, who can let their gardens grow and have same-old sex in the dark, while they are asleep. You realize that while you may have been freed from the washing and the ironing and the domestic slavery that came with your ex and married life, you've really only swapped it for another kind of malevolent sexism. And the worst thing is, this time you booked an appointment and paid for it.

Crimes of Fashion

Losing your fashion mojo

It isn't news that a woman's dress sense can go amiss when she has a baby. Until they confused us all by becoming trendy, 'mum jeans' were a byword for bad fashion. The likes of Stella McCartney and Georgia May Jagger might remember their mothers' wardrobes as a treasure trove of Chloe and Terry de Havilland, but for most of us they were the place where Wallis batwing sweaters went to die.

As a mother, it creeps up on you slowly, this post-partum loss of style. After all, you start with good-enough intentions. Buoyed by pictures of your Gwens and Gwyneths looking hot with a child or two in tow, you tell yourself that there's no reason you too can't keep the side up once the baby's born. True, you might not look so fabulous at the minute, while you're eight months' gone and forty-six stone, but nor are you going to spend the rest of your life in your husband's T-shirts and bobbly leggings that sag at the knees. At least, that's the plan.

Then you have the baby and all bets are off. At this stage of the game, if it goes over your boobs, it goes on. In any case, you tell yourself, it's early days. It doesn't matter if you spend the week wearing the same tracksuit bottoms. You got dressed, didn't you? Christ, there's only so much you can achieve in a day.

Eventually, after what feels like – and indeed is – months, your boobs settle down to something approaching humanoid size and you realize you can't face another day in those tracksuit bottoms and your old maternity vests, even though they now make you feel quite slim – unlike all your other clothes.

But trying on new clothes is still depressing, and you're feeling way too poor to spend money on them. Not that there's any time for shopping, what with all the feeding and the changing and the weeping 'Why didn't you *warn* me?' down the phone at your mother. And all that time you should be drifting around Selfridges, you're actually eating cake in cafes, listening to other women's boring breastfeeding stories so that you can chime in with your own.

It's at this stage that, fashion-wise, you start to lose the plot a bit because practicality has so forcefully entered the equation. A notion you embrace perhaps a bit too enthusiastically as you try to convince yourself that those feeding tops in JoJo Maman Bébé are nice, and that Hooter Hiders are anything other than revolting.

When, finally, you do return to shopping, you break into it gently at Gap, where the sizing is so kind and there always seems to be a sale on. Besides, it sells all the clothes you will ever need for your new life, which is to say it stocks boyfriend jeans, grey T-shirts and navy jumpers. Or even navy T-shirts and grey jumpers. You wear these solidly until the time comes when you're invited to an occasion that calls for something dressier. This is when you wish it was 2006 again and you could trade the T-shirt for a sparkly top and be done with it, as this new fashion is all so baffling, what with the unitards and hiking shoes and garish floral patterns. You find yourself getting offended by fashion barometers as whatever you last bought inevitably features in the 'down' column. And that's when you realize that you've only gone and god-damn done it. You've turned into your mother.

Having a soft spot for catalogues

As a teenager you were so sneery about them – the Kays, Next Directories and Lands' Ends of this world. They were somehow just not cool. They weren't quite there with buying ladies' comfort shoes from the back pages of the *Sunday Telegraph* magazine, but still, something about them said you'd given up.

These days you know that online shopping is where it's at. But as much as you love the internet, ASOS overwhelms you with choice, Net-a-Porter makes the assumption you're a billionaire and everything that arrives from Zara turns out to be horrible. Besides, all you really want is a nice navy jumper. And maybe a white shirt and a jersey dress. Because, the truth is, all your life now calls for is what the magazines describe as 'basics'.

These are easy enough to buy online, but on a website it can be hard to get a clear-enough picture of what the clothes are actually like. Sometimes you just want to see them in print, on a wholesome-looking model. Maybe on a Norfolk beach, with a chocolate Labrador running past.

Now that you don't have the time to schlep around town of a Saturday, it's handy that these catalogues fall out of your copy of *Grazia*. And there seem to be dozens of them, all aimed squarely at you: Hush, Me+Em, Baukjen – each doing their own version of the exact same Breton top. These are the kind of niche, family-run companies that name their dresses Catherine in the hope that the Duchess of Cambridge will wear one and make them all gazillionaires.

Brands like these know that, even in this digital age, the over-thirty-fives love a catalogue. This is partly because they are convenient – you can flick through one while you're waiting for the kettle to boil – but it's also because catalogues are better than websites at selling you a lifestyle. And now that you are too old and tired to have a life, a life*style* is the next best thing.

And it's cunning, what they can do with a decent photographer and a few nice locations. Flick through the Sweaty Betty brochure and you can be persuaded that you're the kind of person who does ballet-barre classes. A few pages on you can convince yourself that the only reason you don't go running after work is because you haven't got a reflective jacket.

The White Company allows you to imagine being that person with the immaculate bed, complete with throw cushions, rather than the woman who doesn't seem to have moved on that far from her futon days. By styling up log cabins, meanwhile, Toast does an impeccable job of making you want to spend £75 on some pyjamas. Yes, you think, looking at a model on a Slovakian mountainside, I really could do with a storm lamp and some bedsocks.

Every one of these shops is more expensive than average, but they have sales. And these days the quality of H&M, Topshop et al makes you go all huffy. Disposable fashion is not for you, thank you very much. You don't buy something on a Saturday afternoon to wear that evening, only to stick it in the back of your wardrobe for ever. You buy something and expect to wear it 60,000 times without it bobbling. You want clothes that wash well, a phrase you didn't even really know the meaning of until you hit thirty. What you want is upmarket quality at a mid-market price; clothing that nods to fashion without being slavish to it. What you want is a catalogue.

Giving your son a look

Most mothers of boys have, however fleetingly, felt disappointed that they will never have the same fun with clothes that mothers of girls get to have. The achingly pretty dresses, the tiny ribbons and bows – as a MOB, these will never be your domain. Not for you the Liberty-print tunics and GapKids designer collaborations. Instead you spend every shopping trip shuffling past the racks of tulle and satin to the tiny rail in the back corner of the shop, where you find two pairs of chinos and a top with a football on it.

But this doesn't mean you have to give up entirely. Even when your son's clothes are mostly hand-me-downs, or gifts that well-meaning relatives insist on buying three sizes too big, it's perfectly possible to give your son a look. These are the most popular options:

1. Little Lord Fauntleroy

See: Prince George, posh people, rich Euros.

What to look for: Old-fashioned bloomers, smocks and rompers, Peter Pan collars, traditional motifs like sailboats and soldiers.

Advantages: Not a hard look to master, once you've found the shops that do this kind of stuff (Trotters, Rachel Riley, basically anywhere in Chelsea).

Disadvantages: Looks faintly ridiculous, especially if you live in a hard northern town; unlikely your son will thank you for all those dress coats/ T-bar shoes in years to come.

2. Mini Pop Star

See: the Stefani–Rossdale children, or indeed most celebrity offspring. Usually goes hand-in-hand with a Travis Bickle haircut and stupid/ made-up name.

What to look for: T-shirts bearing slogans like 'What would Joe Strummer do?', adult trends in miniature (leggings, sweatshirts, leopard print, etc.).

Advantages: A popular option, so no shortage of choice out there; when your son rips his jeans it becomes part of the look.

Disadvantages: Can be expensive/high maintenance; child looks a dick.

3. Dead Rock Star

What to look for: Boys sporting long hair, scruffy Converse, drainpipe jeans, kurtas, beads.

Usually inspired by some rock star the mother had a teenage crush on: Jim Morrison, Michael Hutchence, Kurt Cobain, etc.

Advantages: More socially acceptable than dressing your daughter up as a dead sex symbol.

Disadvantages: Still a bit weird, if you think about it too much.

4. Vintage Child

What to look for: Stripy OshKosh dungarees, seventies hand-knits, T-shirts featuring cartoon characters from your own childhood – Peanuts, Garfield, Noddy, etc.

Advantages: Cheap – eBay, charity shops and market stalls are a mine of this stuff. If your mum kept your old baby clothes, you're laughing. Can tell yourself that your child looks original and unique. Also that you are recycling/avoiding cheap, sweatshop-made clothes, ergo are a better person than everyone else.

Disadvantages: Smug and annoying; also, if you leave your Hackney comfort zone and find your child stood next to a Little Lord Fauntleroy, yours will look a filthy grebo by comparison.

5. Evacuee Child

What to look for: As above, but with a penchant for Fair-Isle tank tops, side partings, Brylcreem, etc.

Advantages: Popular with design-conscious parents – the ones with rockabilly fringes and an exhaustive knowledge of mid-century chairs – as it offers the unique benefit of allowing you to match your children to your furniture. Tells the world that you value heritage, craftsmanship, etc. **Disadvantages:** Like Vintage Child, can be slightly irritating. All those Fair-Isle knits are a bitch to wash.

6. Fancy-dress Child

What to look for: Parents go in for cute animals: think bear, monkey or, in season, reindeer. Others go the comedy route, which usually involves food (pumpkin, hot dog, pea-in-a-pod). Hipster parents tend towards inappropriate references that will be lost on the child (*Edward Scissorhands*, *A Clockwork Orange*, *Breaking Bad*'s Walt and Jesse). But once the child is old enough to have a say, it's fireman or superhero all the way, we're afraid.

Advantages: Having your child wander around dressed as a crocodile for no particular reason makes them look cute and quirky, and you feel all laid-back and Bohemian. You can expect lots of smiles and *aahs* in the street.

Disadvantages: The smiles and *aahs* only come on the costume's first couple of outings, after which your child is just another urchin in manky polyester. Superhero costumes often come with built-in muscle, which can be unnerving. And, like all superheroes, they have their nemesis, which in this case is fire.

7. Dressing your child in charity-shop cast-offs

In itself a statement, one that tells the world you are above dressing your son up as Michael

Hutchence and have better things to spend your money on than children's clothes. Very judgemental and snobby.

That said, some mothers genuinely aren't bothered what their children wear, and would no more dress their son as an evacuee than they would take him to spend the night in Bethnal Green Tube station. You may think you're one of these women. But you probably care more than you think. Often this only becomes clear on those rare occasions when your partner dresses your children. Then you clock the enormous Peppa Pig vest, teamed with the stained tracksuit bottoms you thought you'd chucked months ago, and realize your son has gone beyond badly dressed and entered the realms of *uncared for*. And so you quietly sneak him upstairs and change him into something more acceptable.

Anoraks, trainers, backpacks: your new practical wardrobe

It's not intentional, this tendency to dress like a geography teacher on a Year-8 field trip. But despite your efforts, you end up succumbing. Oh, you start off all right, wearing your nice jeans with a decent pair of shoes – something that might conceivably pass as an 'outfit'. But you get cold, and wet. After all, nobody warned you quite how much time you'd be spending outside, going for long, aimless walks and milling about in playgrounds.

What with all that walking, your shoes start getting shagged, so you decide to save them, if not for 'best', then for 'not trudging through the park'. And while you're at it, there's no point even wearing your good trainers, as some small person will only pour juice on them or make you go the muddy route home.

So you end up wearing your crappy, workaday trainers, the ones you bought before you had the children because you thought you might take up running (ha!). Otherwise you rely on Converse or Superga or some other affordable knockaround shoe that's deemed acceptable, only for the bastard fashion Nazis to then decide they're over. You're past the stage of wearing leather culottes because a magazine tells you to, but if a new style of Nike, Vans or Adidas comes out, you must have them, even if you secretly know they're vile. Because if you can walk five miles in them without getting blisters, frankly they're a winner.

When you come to buy a coat, you find yourself tutting at the too-thin fabrics and impractical colours (Peach? Baby pink? What are they *thinking*?), not to mention the prices. In other words, you find yourself turning into your mother. Since no woman yet has mastered the art of pushing a buggy and holding an umbrella, you embrace the parka, the duffel and any other coat with a built-in hood. In fact, you're all over any trend that happens to be practical, regardless of how ugly it is. Duck boots? They could work. Overpriced wellies? Don't mind if you do. The gilet remains a step too far (although there *is* something appealing about having both a warm chest and the freedom to move your arms). But Barbours, trenches, Canada Goose jackets – anything comfortable and waterproof, in other words – have your name on them.

You've gone from being oblivious to the seasons to noticing little else. In fact, you're in danger of becoming that old person who talks about the weather all the time. While former you would have scoffed at the idea of buying an anorak, new you is coming to terms with the idea that you're still expected to do the school/nursery run *even when it's tipping it down*. So you sell yourself on an anorak, either by buying a posh one from somewhere like Seasalt or Petit Bateau, or by going to Topshop and telling yourself that it's 'festivalwear'. In winter you wear a bobble hat, and on colder days you contemplate giving up altogether and only ever shopping in Cotswold Outdoor.

Handbags, meanwhile, must be big enough to hold nappies, wipes and a thousand plastic sachets of half-crushed oatcakes. No more frivolous clutches or cross-body purses for you. Totes are one thing, but the backpack is a revelation, allowing you to push a buggy *and* hold a coffee at the same time. That's one trend you won't be letting go of easily.

In summer you dig out those short, pretty tea dresses you used to wear – the ones you hoped made you look a bit like Kate Moss – only to discover that one tussle with a toddler and the park's your gynaecologist. Denim shorts are the way forward (assuming you can find them in a forgiving mid-thigh length), or better still, all-in-ones (though these come with their own loo-related issues, along with that unfortunate affliction we like to call 'long bum'). Your leather jacket gets relegated to child-free days, thanks to its inability to cope with a sudden downpour, and you find yourself embracing a uniform of sweatshirt, T-shirt and jeans.

Sadly, this is where it can all go wrong. The boyfriend/girlfriend/mum jean, that expensive-tracksuit thing calling itself 'sports luxe' – these are trends that seem perfectly pitched at mothers. But don't fall for them. Because unless you wear that sportswear with a four-inch heel, you just look depressed. Most of the new jean styles also demand high-maintenance footwear and it's way too much to think about, on top of everything else.

Easier, then, just to look like a geography teacher.

Changing Relations

Engaging in competitive tiredness

Of all the horrible, repetitive, boring arguments you will have with your partner, the one that will most make you want to stove in your own brain is the one about which of you is tireder.

The boring truth is that one of you will have had a better night's sleep than the other. If you managed it, then high five. But it's a Pyrrhic victory as you'll be living with a dog-tired person who's nothing but vile to you all day. The next night it'll be his turn to sleep in, which means you'll be exhausted and spend the day being foul to him. And so the whole sorry cycle continues. For one of you to get a good night's sleep, the other has to suffer, and it turns out you have to be Joan of Arc to do that silently.

Because no one can definitively prove they are more tired, the argument can degenerate quickly into pettiness. And neither party is above lying. 'I was up three times in the night.' 'Well, I was up four.' (No one can remember how many times they were up, it just feels like it was bloody loads.) If this fails, you can play the memory-loss card: 'I was so tired today, I forgot about *insert important engagement here*. My short-term memory is shot to pieces.'

If that doesn't work, you may find yourself resorting to the descent-into-madness line ('I'm so tired I feel like I'm losing my mind'). Or its close relative, 'I can't cope.' The winner is usually whoever can take it furthest, with extra points netted for tears and claims that you're about to be fired/sectioned, etc.

As with so many post-baby arguments, it boils down to this: who has it harder? Which is more difficult, being knackered at home with a baby or being knackered at work with coffee and adult company on tap? Naturally there are jobs where being at work is undoubtedly more challenging. If your partner works down a mine, say, or in a Calcutta sewer, he probably has this one nailed. But for 98.7 per cent of the population, work involves a lot of Facebook, a bit of eBay and a little are-you-watching-*House-of-Cards*? as you wait for the kettle to boil. There are stresses, sure, and, Christ knows, no shortage of dull meetings. But the notion that doing a bit of graphic design or telesales or whatever is somehow harder than dealing with a colicky baby round the clock is an insult. Men know this too – after all, you'll notice they're not exactly beating down our doors to do it.

When you've had enough of the who-has-it-tougher argument, you might find yourself progressing to a more general who-does-more debate. Car tax, insurance payments, laundry, supermarket shopping – all those boring life-admin tasks can be strung into an endless tit-for-tat row about who works harder for this family.

Other offshoots of the argument include: Who Looks

More Haggard? Who Has More Time to Exercise? and Who Sees Less of Their Friends? In fact, there are so many variations on the theme that, with a little practice, you can soon be having no other conversation at all. Indeed, many couples quickly reach this goal (42 per cent, if the stats are to be believed).

So how do you avoid it? That's tricky. Often it's a question of knowing the flashpoints and steering clear of them. This means never mentioning how tired you are, even if you're after support and sympathy, or perhaps an hour off. Because in response you'll only hear how knackered he is, and how he was up working until midnight while you crashed at 10 p.m. with *Homes & Antiques* on your lap. Although if he says he's tired and you try the same trick, don't be surprised if he sighs and says, 'It's not a competition, you know.'

Sometimes it's even worth conceding, 'Yes, you are tireder,' just for a quiet life. But it's only a temporary reprieve because tomorrow it starts all over again.

Only ever going on girls' nights out

It's not that you don't like girls. You are a girl, after all. Your best friend is a girl. And your mum and your daughter and your sister – all of them your top favourite people in the world. You are totally down with the whole being a girl, hanging out with girls thing. Girls, yay, woo-hoo!

But during the baby years, and for most of the years after, it can seem as though all the men in the world have disappeared. Life feels like the bit after dinner in *Downton*

Abbey, when the men hole up in the dining room and get stuck into the port and cigars, while you're left sitting fireside with Grandma, drinking sherry and doing the sewing.

The world becomes resolutely feminine: you're surrounded by midwives and nurses, mothers and grandmas. Other mums, mums, mums everywhere. And you love your lady friends. You bare your soul to those chicks, sob on their sick-stained shoulders, tell them all about the sorry state of your post-natal labia. But you do sometimes wonder what happened to all the boys.

Sure, you interface with males at dinner parties and kids' parties and all the other nice social gatherings. But there are unwritten rules at play here, about how much chatting is acceptable with Other People's Husbands. Generally speaking, you're OK with questions about home improvements (solar panels, underfloor heating, etc.) or his work. Feel free to talk for as long as you like about your own home improvements – planning permission/extensions are always safe ground, as are the kids and/or your husband's work. Stick to DIY, kids and work. Under no circumstances go off-script or share too much personal information (that's for the woman to find out from you, and tell him about later). Don't laugh too hard at his jokes either or spend too long talking directly to him. Definitely never get his number. And probably best not to make friends on Facebook.

You fully understand this logic. You are all paid-up on this front. After all, you don't really like it when women talk to your other half for too long. You know he's definitely not that funny, so why is old too-much-make-up-on over there pissing herself at him?

But even though you subscribe to these rules of play, you can't help feeling a bit rose-tinted about the old days, when you used to have friends who were boys, as well as girls. When you could text a male friend, go for a pint with him, meet him at the shops – do all sorts of non-sexy things with him – and no one cared.

Because even though you spend pretty much every waking hour complaining about the one you live with, you sometimes miss the company of men. The uncomplicated, straightforward nature of it. The lack of rivalry and insecurity. The way you don't have to spend twenty minutes paying each other compliments and discussing outfits before having a real conversation. Not having real conversations at all, but ones about which 1980s metal band you'd be, if you had to be a 1980s metal band (Manowar, obvs). The smut and the swearing, drinking games and kebabs after the pub. And, yes, the flirting. That little tug of sexual tension, even if you didn't fancy them a jot. It was life-affirming and fun hanging out with boys. They used to be a big part of your life.

You can't honestly say you miss kebabs any more – not interested unless they come from Waitrose in some posh marinade. But you can't help feeling that, somehow, nights out just seem a bit lacking.

Because now you only ever go on Girls' Nights Out. These are the nights where you're going out, but not to a dinner party or some other gathering where it's socially acceptable to talk (on script) to Other People's Husbands. They are the birthday drinks, the book-club nights and the NCT-mums get-togethers. The school-mums Christmas dos and the try-the-new-place meals. These nights are great and good – you're the first to sign up – but they are always Girls Only.

Admittedly, one of the main reasons for this is the babysitting issue. (Why pay someone else to stay in when one of you can?) And with a babysitter comes the stress of having to buy them Maltesers and make it look as though the kids do get a wash occasionally. And you have to spend the rest of the weekend worrying about whether you really did ask her if she could get any E, when you came in all shit-faced.

But mostly these evenings are Girls Only for the simple reason that that's what happens now. As a mother and a partner, you sign an unwritten contract that says you promise not to hang out with boys who aren't your husband any more, no matter how innocent your intentions. (This is even truer for single mums, who are never allowed in the same room as other people's unchaperoned husbands. The only men they're allowed to fraternize with are the ones in cyberspace, or else the unknowns in the pub, who may or may not also be married.)

Another reason these occasions can seem a little unfamiliar is that in the time you were out of action popping sprogs, the night-out-scape changed. They had a revamp, switched the set. In ye olden days, you'd happily spend hours around a table in any scuzzy old boozer, drinking pints of lager-top and smoking Marlboro Lights, flicking your ash in your empty pork scratchings packet and getting off with whoever was sitting next to you. You were either wearing what you'd been in all day at work or something that hadn't seen the washing machine for some time.

These days a Girls' Night Out requires getting dressed

up in that middle-ground sort of way – typically skinny jeans, heels and a top that isn't a T-shirt, ideally with some sort of shimmery thread through it. It involves eating out because, hey, we're all foodies now. And going somewhere sophisticated, drinking cocktails, because they're a treat. And we're all about treats to self, now that we're mothers. There's nothing intrinsically wrong with any of this, but it can feel a bit prescriptive, like you're in your own Barbie 'Girls' Night Out' set. And look, here's Ken the waiter with the Amaretto Sours!

There's not much you can do about this state of affairs. You can't exactly start inviting single men along to your book-club night out just to make it less boring. Or worse, inviting your friend's husband out for your birthday and not her, because he's way more fun. Insist too hard that the husbands come along every time and you start to sound like a woman with an ulterior motive.

No, you must accept your fate and be grateful that you have girlfriends, and that you are going out at all. It won't be long before you can't even drink at home watching *X-Factor*, because you have to pick up your drunk daughter from town at midnight. She's waiting outside the kebab shop.

Being chippy about your in-laws

This a difficult section to write. The in-laws might be reading this. Or at least they are supposed to be. If they never mention this bit, we'll know they haven't read it. And that will be another black mark in their book. They can't win, basically.

That's the thing: it's not so much that you dislike them in the way that, say, you might the kid who is mean to yours at school. It's more that you can't shake the feeling that everything is the in-laws' fault. When the breast milk turns sour and you realize what a shit deal you get in this whole thing, they begin to represent everything that is wrong in your life.

Because, let's face it, whether you are still with him or not, if they hadn't had that man – the one who got you pregnant – and brought him up in that funny way so he did all those irritating things, none of this would have happened.

It's a shame because it started so well. They seemed so nice. The sort of family you wished you'd had instead of your own, all fun and cool and interesting. They welcomed you with loving arms: his mum was your new BFF, his sister your new confidante. His brother may even have flirted with you. His dad, too. At least that's what it looked like he was trying to do. It was all long Sunday lunches and overly generous Christmas presents and showing you off at family weddings.

But there's nothing like sharing a gene pool to bring some dark, visceral shit to the surface. And unless you lucked out by marrying the only man on the planet whose mother thinks that you have it harder than she did, there is trouble ahead.

Because that's what they all think: that they had it tougher than you. That they worked longer hours, had fewer dishwashers, lower expectations about holidays and had certainly never heard of 'me time'. They never bought themselves new clothes, always dressed the children in hand-me-downs, cut their hair around a bowl and did all the rest of that we-were-poor-but-happy stuff they like to pump out over dinner.

Actually, they probably don't think this at all. They probably couldn't give a monkey's about who had it harder, and are actually thinking about where they'll buy their next holiday home or how to spend your husband's inheritance before you get your mitts on it. But even if this who-had-it-harder stuff is a construct in your crazy, sleep-deprived mind – that's what you'll think they think.

And the implication – as you like to rant to your own (by default) saintly mother, and increasingly to your husband, because you have started to care less about hurting his feelings – is that you are somehow having an easy ride. That you are kicking back at the soft-play centre (something else they never had, because of course children played in the street in those days), having a right old laugh. As if you would actually choose to be there, in a room with no windows that smells of shit in scented nappy bags.

The indignation you feel – the injustice of it all – whether born of fact or fiction, begins to set in deep. And eventually everything they say and do is read with your new indignant glasses on, heard through your new indignant headphones. Inviting you for lunch, once a welcome gesture, is now a way to highlight how rubbish you are at cooking. The presents they give the children are now loaded statements about how much you spoil them, or else a reminder of their terrible taste. The continual administering of sweets and treats is not a grandparent's right, it's a flagrant disregard for your wishes.

Every annoying thing your partner does – his apparent ignorance of the toilet brush, the way he scrapes the butter from the knife back into the dish with bits of toast in it AS IF YOU ARE GOING TO USE IT – it's all their fault now. Your indignant mind knows this to be true. And eventually the indignation becomes the status quo, and an ancient ritual – the bashing of the in-laws – is maintained.

And you realize this is why there are so many jokes about mothers-in-law. Everyone gets moody with their in-laws. And when feminism finally puts as many women comics on the stage as men, it won't mean the end of the mother-in-law gag so much as the rise of the one-about-my-father-in-law.

'Mum friends' and other boring people

If you're lucky, you will have your baby at the same time as your friends, who will all happen to live within a one-mile radius of your house. If you live in the real world, however, all your friends will be caught up in exciting and hectic careers, or will have had their babies long ago and moved to the end of the earth. As the demands of a baby mean you'll now be socializing at off-peak hours (9.30 a.m. on a Tuesday, anyone?), the result is that you need to make some new friends, and fast.

The most forward-thinking types pay to do this at NCT. For the less-organized ones, it's a case of standing at the sidelines of toddler groups and accepting that, while your life was once varied and interesting, it's now about singing 'Sleeping Bunnies' at the local children's centre while nobody talks to you. To top it off, in society's eyes you have become 'woman who spends her days at toddler groups', a figure offered about as much status as 'woman who spends her days in the cemetery shouting at pigeons'.

And the whole making-friends malarkey is *hard*. Which is strange, because it's not as if your standards are particularly high any more. Once the qualities you looked for in a friend were humour and intelligence, kindness, the willingness to have a good time. Your new criteria are geography, availability and children roughly the same age as yours. These days you'd be mates with Myra Hindley if she offered you a coffee and listened while you cried about your husband using work as an excuse not to get up in the night as much as you do.

With any luck, you will find some people you can have a latte with. But these new mum friends come with two major downsides. One, you're always sober when you see them. This can make for stilted conversation, particularly when your only common ground is the children. And, inevitably, they are all you talk about.

Sometimes that's OK (i.e. when it's your own child you're talking about), but there's also the mother who insists on sharing her kid's every foible – characteristics that strike you as common to children the world over ('She runs everywhere,' 'He just *loves* sultanas') – and you find yourself stuck in the most boring conversation anyone's ever had, ever.

These new friends also have a habit of bringing your shallower instincts to the fore. 'She looks so old!' you think of a mother at the church playgroup, forgetting that you spent the morning Googling retinol creams, and that your anti-Botox stance has more to do with the fact that you can't afford it than any genuine objection to injecting poison into your face. 'And why is she wearing that? Is she depressed?' you wonder, a bit rich considering you're in the same jeans you've been sporting for days, and the closest you've come to washing your hair is dousing it in Batiste.

But your fellow mums do have one thing going for them, namely that they're free for an hour between the lunchtime nap and teatime. And it's not as if you're offering up your most fascinating self, either. After all, you've got to tell someone about that rash your child had (the one you thought was meningitis, but wasn't). And who else are you going to share this with? Your real friends? They'd be asleep before you'd finished the sentence. Or, more likely, they'd smile and nod, before telling all your mutual friends what a baby bore you've become. So with your real friends, you listen to their stories and pretend you've been out more than you really have. And with your new mum friends, you talk about Sudocrem and that article they read that said day care gives children cancer.

But these new friendships aren't all bad news. It's fun to test the waters to see how wild (or otherwise) these women were in their previous lives. And it's rewarding when you break down the barrier and go out with them in the evening for the first time. This is when you see them with lipstick on and discover there's more to them than the tired-looking drudge you see pushing a buggy around town.

With any luck, you'll go from talking about sleep training to something more interesting, such as which husband you'd most like to have an affair with. If it goes badly, you'll still be talking about the kids. In which case it's back to square one, and you'll need to find yourself some new new friends.

Becoming bad cop

You totally had designs on being the fun parent. You'd be all about popcorn at the movies, theme-park trips, the odd matinee musical. Yeah, our mum, she's such a laugh, they'd think. Always smiling, ever the joker.

But, annoyingly, it doesn't seem to pan out that way. Instead you're the one going on at them to brush their teeth, banning dolls that look like hookers and putting your foot down when they want to watch sixteen hours of *Adventure Time*. It's you who gets arsey about the iPad and frets about the sugar content of raisins.

You didn't want to be that person – the dullard, the dag, the one who wants to quietly bin their Easter eggs and gets nervous when they ride their dad's shoulders. Sometimes it feels like you're on your own, like it's just you who worries about their future dental health, while your partner would let them play with a pit bull if it meant he got an extra hour in bed. All too often it can seem like he's on a mission to be Disney Dad, all rough 'n' tumble and trips to the ice-cream van, while you're there moaning about manners and setting rules about when they're allowed to leave the table.

There's a reason for this, which is that you're the one who cares more about this stuff. Just like if you didn't buy the Christmas presents, no one would get anything, so you get stuck with most of the discipline. This is because, when it comes down to it, you're the one most affected by your kids' bad behaviour. It's you who squirms with embarrassment when they tell your friend to shut up or throw themselves screaming to the floor because someone else won musical chairs. Likewise, it's you who panics if they're late for karate or turn up for the school trip without a packed lunch.

Because, the world being the way it is, it's likely that you're the one who oversees their lives and schedules. Regardless of who's at home most, it's you who ends up in charge. Not because you want to do it all, but because you can't bear not doing it all. Which is kind of a tricky position, when you think about it.

It doesn't help that, as mothers, we're judged so often. If your child behaves horribly in public, people tend to give you that smile – the one that says, 'manage your child'. When that child's with its father, they're too busy thinking what a hero he is to notice the tantrum. Were they to judge his parenting skills, it's unlikely he could care less, while you – tired, insecure wreck that you are – swing between fury and despair at any perceived disapproval. Being judged makes you paranoid about your mothering skills, and it's hard to be the fun parent when you're stressing. Frankly, it's no wonder you don't want to go to bleeding Chessington.

This desire to be seen as a good parent is also what lands you the role of bollocker-in-chief. Which means that you end up dishing out the bulk of the tellings-off. Meanwhile their dad gets to breeze in late and toss his squealing children in the air, like James Stewart in *It's a Wonderful Life*, as you stand around like a pillock, worrying that it's way past bedtime and they'll be knackered and vile in the morning.

Come morning, it's you who's tearing around the house, panicking that they're late for school or nursery. Because you know there'll be some mealy little punishment – a late ticket here, a pointed remark there – which your partner will disregard, but you will see as a sign that everyone thinks you are one of those flaky, chaotic mothers your own mum used to gossip about.

Which is a bummer, since you're also the one who gets to make sure they've had a haircut and cut their nails, buy their shoes and do a whole list of other tasks too much of a yawn to mention. So not only do you get to do all the grunt work, you end up being the monster as well. Occasionally you may try and reverse the roles and relax. But by now you're so conditioned it's practically impossible to let go, and you find yourself wincing as they shove another HobNob into their mouths before lunch.

But there is good news! There is a solution. And this is to have more children. Because if you've got more than three there's no way you can be stressing about whether they've all eaten their vegetables or done their reading. Being neurotic is a privilege only afforded to mothers with one or two. More than that and you simply don't have the time. So there's your answer – have five kids. It's the only way you'll ever get to relax.

Losing all your friends

Back when you were child-free and friends announced they were having babies, a part of you would be pleased for them, but another would be sad and disappointed, because you knew that you were losing a partner in crime. You knew this spelled the end of wild nights out, and that all future meet-ups would have to be scheduled three weeks in advance and take place near her new house in Zone 70.

Then, when the baby was born, although you enjoyed having the opportunity to go and buy cute stuff at Baby Gap, another part of you felt like Patsy in *Ab Fab* and wanted to hiss at it for monopolizing the conversation, even though it had naff-all to say. You would share something important and heartfelt with your friend, eager for her advice, only to watch her fuss over the baby and say, 'Sorry, what was that?' After repeating yourself forty-six times, you'd leave, feeling like the whole visit had been massively unsatisfactory *and hadn't involved any drinking at all.*

After that, she'd take weeks to return a call or email, and when she finally did get round to doing so, would breezily mention how busy she'd been. Even though you were putting in ten hours a day at some shitty office across town and couldn't so much as find time to get your eyebrows done, and she wasn't even working. At the time you might even have said (oh, the shame of it!), 'But what do you *do* all day?' And there was a silence, which you filled by back-pedalling like mad and mumbling something like,

'God, babies. Must be manic. Hardest job in the world,' etc., while secretly thinking she was making a bit of a meal of changing a few nappies and going to Gymboree.

So . . . mothers. You knew they made shit friends. And you also knew that, if/when you had kids, you would not make their mistakes. You would not assume that anyone outside your immediate family wanted to hear about that thing your kid did. You would know that, when people asked after your children, they wanted a five-word précis, max. And you certainly wouldn't leave every dinner at a lame-arsed 10.30 p.m. because you'd got to get back for the babysitter. You would be a proper friend, like you were before – not this person who turns up late, leaves early and says nothing interesting in between.

But then you have your baby and realize all at once why your mum friends never called you. You learn about the witching hour – that period between 5 p.m. and 7 p.m. when you lock yourself in the bathroom to send your partner a series of increasingly homicidal texts. And when the baby finally goes to sleep and at last you have ten seconds to yourself, the last thing you feel like is a chirpy telephone catch-up. Before you know it, you find that the most convenient time to talk to anyone is 7 a.m. on a Sunday morning, when – guess what? – nobody wants to speak to you.

It's around this time that you find yourself seeing less of your old crowd. People move to other towns or start staying in themselves. And suddenly you're of an age where you don't run into people in bars at the weekend. The friends you do see, you've arranged to meet, and you do this in increasingly select groups, round at each other's houses, where there isn't much scope for meeting anyone new. Not that you have time for new friends. You can barely keep in touch with the old ones. People who used to know your every quandary now hear from you once a year, when you write 'Happy birthday, lady!!!' on their timeline.

It's sad, and you miss them. The months roll on, and gradually you find people who are willing to babysit. And slowly it reaches a point where you can stay up past 10 p.m. without passing out in your pudding. But by that point, you realize that it's been too long, and you're not even sure who to call.

Going it alone

He's been seeing another woman. Or maybe you have. He's spent all the money. You're not the person you used to be. He drinks too much. You definitely do. Whatever the reason for your split, waking up single – and a mum – after all these years as half of a couple, is quite a thing. Married or divorced, living together or separated – it's a time of low self-esteem and high self-discovery. Of joy and pain. Love and loss. Wine and fags.

It's hard to summarize the kaleidoscope of new realities that make up the deal now you're a single mum. But some truths ring loud and clear for many of us:

On mess: You are not, as you've been insisting for some years now, a zen goddess whose tidy nature has been crushed by the man-beast you've been living with. You're pretty messy, actually. In fact, you're a pig. The good news is that, with only yourself to huff and mutter at, you forget to be pissed off about it and elect to watch *The Affair* box set instead. You are a happy pig.

On weight: You instantly lose half a stone by not preparing big evening meals. Obviously you eat, and you feed the kids. But they're getting a hot lunch at school and only need a light supper, you tell yourself. And can you be arsed mashing potatoes and chopping carrots every night? Boiled eggs – and other foods requiring no preparation or washing-up – become your best friends. You grieve for the hours of your life you spent making curry pastes from scratch, when all along you could have been eating avocados.

On finances: Unless you are Heather Mills-McCartney, you will feel a degree of pinch now that you're a single mother. Enjoying the martyrdom that comes with the territory, you pick up green-looking ham in the reduced aisle at Waitrose and revisit charity shops, telling yourself that you'd forgotten how much you love vintage. You batch-cook cauldrons of dhal, and eBay your son's old football trainers instead of passing them on to neighbours. With tears of desperation in your voice, you implore the children not to waste shampoo in the bath, as you work hard to pay for that stuff. And you encourage them to save for the family holiday with one of those money boxes you can only open with a tin-opener. You do all these bleeding-heart things, and then spend your child benefit on a £200 denim jacket from MiH, because you're miserable and deserve a treat. And no one else is going to buy it for you.

On child welfare: The kids are all right. The kids are fine. They're doing great. Practise different ways to say this over and over in cheery tones, because 'How are the kids?'

is, without exception, the one question everyone asks. Largely it is heartfelt and without agenda. But some can't help doing the 'concerned' face, to remind you that you could be screwing up your children's lives. Have some divorce statistics handy ('Did you know that 42 per cent of UK marriages end in divorce? That's almost half of us.') You might also politely remind them that married people do quite well at screwing up their kids, too. 'Look at you!' you might say if you're feeling bold, or drunk (90 per cent more likely at any time of day now you are separated).

On friendship: Your friends offer their unequivocal support, mostly by drinking wine with you and trying to make you go on Tinder. But it's important to remember that this is your midlife crisis, not theirs, and they probably couldn't think of anything worse than going to that middle-aged 'club night' at the Masonic Hall where everyone smells of patchouli. Actually, nor could you. Also, inexplicably, you never see any of their husbands again. Ever.

On being an independent, single lady: You can change the bulb in a spotlight and put air in the car tyres. Uh-huh, honey, yes you can. But don't expect these events to be rewarding feminist moments. It's not called Do It Yourself for nothing.

On your mother: Your mother won't approve of your separation, especially if she thinks a man is a good catch because he can change a nappy. She also says, out loud, the words that others dare not, such as: 'He'll get snapped up,' and, 'No one will want you with two children.' Forgive her. She does not understand.

On your ex: You may imagine a fresh, mature and calm relationship blossoming between you and your ex, now that you're free from all that domestic grief. On good days this may even happen. But mostly he will still be your ex, with all the irritating foibles he's always had. And you will still be you, with your unrealistic expectations and destructive hormonal schedule. And you will still come to blows and say vile, hurtful things to each other. Only now you'll do it on the doorstep or in the Co-op car park or wherever you are exchanging the children, instead of in the privacy of your own home.

On the shelf: You give more consideration than is appropriate to a woman of your grey matter to the way you look. You spend much of your new-found free time gazing in disbelief at your wilting form in the mirror, and Googling Botox. Trying to keep the arse from the floor, you do more spinning classes in the first six months of being single than you did in your entire married life. You obsess about your profile picture on every social-media network you use. You analyse your online-dating profile so often, you know the words by heart.

Onwards and upwards: There are times, when the children are with their father and the house is empty, and no one has called or texted to see how you are because they have their own busy and stressful lives, that your heart stops beating with the fear. The fear of what's to become of you, now that you've wandered so far from the pages of your fairy tale. This is when your sock drawer comes into its own. Set to and sort it. Sort every drawer and re-organize every cupboard and don't stop until they get back, and the house is full of noise and chaos, and you wish they'd all bugger off again and leave you alone.

Finding out that your child is autistic

It's only when your son is diagnosed that you discover you have a lot of misconceptions about autism. It turns out, for example, that it doesn't mean being a bit awkward at parties but a whiz at maths. Nor does it mean he'll be one of those kids who draw hyper-detailed landscapes from memory and make you all a fortune, or who can recite any number from the phone book in a way you're not entirely sure how to monetize but still sounds like kind of a cool skill. It turns out that only 1 in 200 autists have any savant ability. Meanwhile, 40 per cent never learn to speak at all, and only 15 per cent will ever hold down a full-time job.

It's the speech and language therapist who first spots it. You have turned up to the drop-in clinic because the people at nursery, who last week were saying that it's fine he can't talk and boys are often a bit slow – 'Did you know Einstein didn't talk until he was four?' – have changed their stance. They are now gently recommending that you get him checked out.

So here you are at the local children's centre, where the SLT is asking you lots of pointed questions about his behaviour and how much he likes technology. Yes, now that she mentions it, he is very fond of the washing machine. And lifts – he loves a lift. Could ride those things all day. And then something clicks and you see where this is heading.

'Do you think he's on the spectrum?' you ask, thinking no such thing yourself because he's so smiley and affectionate, and doesn't stare blankly at the wall in the way that you assume autistic children do.

'Let's not diagnose him now,' she says cheerfully.

Oh.

You go home and consult Dr Google, who offers a checklist of symptoms. How's his eye contact? Autistic children often have poor or no eye contact. Does he answer to his name? Not always, no. But you assumed he was a dreamer or maybe a bit deaf. 'Have you ever had his hearing checked out?' is the next question.

Does he point? Apparently children with autistic spectrum disorder don't. You can't remember ever seeing him point. But you can't remember if he doesn't point either. He walks on tiptoe, which has always bothered you, and it turns out this can be another sign. (The physio told you it was because he's double-jointed, which again is common in children with autism. As is a fondness for Thomas the Tank Engine. You are screwed.) You're not sure if he hand-flaps, but that thing he does when he's excited – could that be . . .? You realize that you have ticked almost everything on the list.

You whisk him off to a Harley Street paediatrician and speech therapist, because grand gestures like this make you feel like you are doing the best by your child. The speech therapist subjects him to a lot of tests – inset puzzles, pointing out the duck, that kind of thing – which you watch him fail. The paediatrician, who looks eighty if he's a day, says, 'Meh, he could be autistic, but what d'you want a label for?' and tells your son off for touching his phone.

His parting words are, 'We take credit cards.' You learn that Harley Street and expensive does not necessarily mean good.

The NHS paediatrician is way more thorough, but doesn't tell you much, only that because it's being diagnosed so young (he's two and a half), it is 'not mild'. But you are not alone. One in a hundred UK children are diagnosed with autism. When you consider that four times as many boys as girls are diagnosed, that's one in . . . It's a lot of boys. There is no cure, and there is no treatment, although you do qualify for queue-jumper tickets at Legoland. Every cloud.

Beyond a diagnosis, there's not much the NHS can offer, bar some speech-and-language sessions and a parenting course that has a year-long waiting list. The doctors can't tell you what he'll be like aged seven or seventeen because every autistic child is affected differently and their progress varies wildly. All you do know is that it's a lifelong condition. Children with autism become adults with autism. Those milestones many people take for granted – going to university, getting married, having children – will likely never happen for him.

It's the uncertainty that is hardest to deal with, though the tantrums come a close second – terrible twos plus an inability to communicate is an explosive combination. But for the most part he's still very smiley and affectionate. And in any case you don't want to lose hope because, to quote one of the cheesy American books you buy, 'with no hope there is no action,' and you need to do something.

So it's back to Dr Google, who, it turns out, has all

manner of miracle cures. You like to think you are too savvy to fall for internet snake oil, but the websites and testimonials are more convincing than you'd think, and you are a desperate parent, which means that your critical faculties are at least 70 per cent less effective than they were. Even so, you are amazed by the scope of the bullshit on offer. There is chelation therapy, where your son can be injected with ethylene diamine tetra-acetic acid to remove the heavy metals from his blood. He can have vitamin B12 injections and start a detoxification programme. No shortage of people promise that he will be fine if he drinks camel's milk.

But you do come across a couple of sensible – scientifically proven! – interventions that have a good chance of improving your son's prognosis. Known as behavioural therapies, they are more about education than medicine, and involve a lot of one-on-one intensive play sessions. The downside is that they require serious time – some twenty-plus hours a week. If you're going to do it yourself, you'll have to give up work. If you're going to pay someone else to do it, you'll need to find their annual salary. Knowing you've got to throw everything at the wall, you remortgage, aware that this makes you one of the lucky ones.

Finding the right person to come and do the therapy is another hurdle. You lose track of how many candidates traipse through the front door. You are warned that – being private and therefore unregulated – the field attracts some funny people, and you should check police records carefully as this is a dream career for anyone wanting some alone time with children. One woman you interview is part of what you later find out is a cult. Another has a conviction for fraud. A third starts, but then cancels because she's due in court after a fall-out with a neighbour.

You get past the depressed stage, although it's still hard not to be angry. You swear you'll go for the next person who tells you that Einstein didn't talk until he was four. But things get better. Once you have a strategy in place, you start to see progress. He goes from only saying 'hi' and 'bye' to having a list of words. And it's still early days.

It remains impossible to look ahead – who knows what kind of school he'll need or whether he'll ever get to live an independent life? But you remember that uncertainty is rife for everyone, and some of the best people you know didn't go to university or get married or have children. And, as people keep reminding you, he's still the same lovely boy he was.

'No pressure, honest!' Being forced to attend your friends' selling parties

It's the invitation you dread more than an ex-boyfriend's wedding. 'I'm having a little coffee morning. Nothing formal – just a chance for some of the girls to get together, have some cake and maybe buy a couple of things.'

Buy a couple of things? You hope she is having a house sale – you've had your eye on her dining chairs for ages. But, no. Instead she starts raving about some company you've dimly heard of, and how it does the most amazing jewellery/handbags/sex toys and here you are with this fabulous opportunity to buy it all, so that she can earn some commission.

As shopping experiences go, it's down there with a bank-holiday bonanza at B&Q. But at least B&Q is pleasantly impersonal. This is the opposite, which is hell for you, especially if you're the kind of person who avoids boutiques because being alone with a sales assistant makes you feel pressured into buying something. You avoid building relationships with shop owners because it means you won't ever be able to pop in for a browse. Which makes going to a shop where the sales lady is one of your best friends a personal nightmare.

The thing is, you have every sympathy with your friend. She is nervous and needs you, and you can see why. The only thing less fun than going to one of these things must be hosting one. You know she needs cash and that, having been out of the career game a while, her opportunities are in as short supply as her confidence. If her friends don't come along, she doesn't make any money. Your friend's finances are therefore in your hands.

But you're just as skint, and need this about as much as you need one of the tinny-looking charm necklaces she'll be flogging. Even the social aspect of it is not fun, being as how it's going to take place on a weekday morning with a bunch of other women you know, but not well enough to have a good time with.

It's at times like this that you wish you were male. When did you last hear of a bloke hosting a direct-selling party for his closest chums? Would the men do it, as Caitlin Moran would say? As with five-inch stilettos and putting up with lower pay, the answer is a fat resounding *no*. These direct-selling parties are exploitative bullshit that prey on a woman's politeness and inability to leave a place without buying something. What's more, the only people really making money from them are the anonymous corporations behind the whole set-up. In fact, now that you think about it properly, the whole thing reeks.

Which leaves you with four options. These are:

1. **Make up a prior engagement.**
   Effective but unsupportive and your friend will know you are lying.

2. **Go, and buy the smallest, cheapest thing there as a sign of support.**
   Again, everyone there will see through this. Your friend will feel patronized and embarrassed, and you will feel robbed. Good luck with this, in any case. Once you're there, you're in. It's like committing to a cosmetics-counter makeover – no matter how firmly you resolve not to buy anything, you will be upsold.

3. **Go, but accidentally arrive an hour late, by which time the sales rep will have put away her tat and you will be off the hook.**
   This approach seems ingenious but is actually a disaster, as you will learn when the sales rep then unpacks every last thing for your benefit, leaving you obliged to buy extra rubbish to make up for the fact that you've put her out.

4. **Go, and allow yourself to be talked into all manner of crap you will later regret.**
This is what always happens.

Being annoyed with your parents for getting old

One of the many epiphanies you have as a new mother is the one where you realize that your parents went through everything you're going through. There you are, high on all those love hormones, and it dawns on you that your mother must have felt the same thing for you, all those years ago. She must have loved you as fiercely, fed you in the night as wearily, carried you around with as much stoic devotion.

You contemplate this with a mixture of joy and crashing guilt because you never truly understood until now the depth of feeling a parent could have for a child. You imagine them exhausted and uncertain, like you. Damn it, you understand their sacrifices. And you get weepy and want to thank them for everything they did. It's all rather emotional, really. And much too cheesy to say out loud.

Besides, you're busy making your own sacrifices right now. And your parents do seem gratifyingly keen to help you with the baby. Which you get them to do quite a lot, as it goes. You take full advantage of their devotion. Occasionally you wonder if you ask too much of them. But they love it, right? And there's always someone else's mother doing more. You know of someone's mum who travels from Newcastle to Exeter every week to look after the child, so her daughter can go to work. The economics of that can't be right, surely? Another grandmother looks after her granddaughter full-time because the mum is a drug addict. See? You're not that bad.

Then one day you get a little shock when you see your mum and dad. You open the door to them – maybe they've driven for three hours to stay overnight so that you can go to the cinema – and, holy shit, if they haven't grown old.

You phone your siblings to see if they knew about this. Have you seen how old they are? When did this happen? Something must be done. You thought they were bubbling away in the background, preserved in parental aspic. But someone has clearly left the lid off. And, on cue, the oldness begins to spread. Age spots show up everywhere.

They tell you the same stories over and over, twittering on in a way you're sure they never used to. It's almost always about their friends or some other people you don't know. When they call, you do that comedy thing of holding the phone away and pulling a face to your husband, while your mum delivers a stream of consciousness on Harry-from-the-barber's keyhole surgery, and Christine-whose-daughter-is-a-barrister, who's looking for a new house with a bigger garden, but can't find anything she likes.

They become obsessed with journeys and cars, traffic and the price of petrol. They collect coupons and know how many gallons to the dozen their car does. They spend a lot of time worrying about tyre pressure. And parking. Is the parking expensive? What if they can't find a space? They plan routes, and even do practice runs. Practice runs!

They start to forget names. Paperwork and keys get lost. They never answer the phone because, despite what they say, they are definitely going deaf. Have you had your hearing checked? What's that? You linger over the adverts in the back of the Sunday supplements. Gloria Hunniford enters a walk-in bath in a swimsuit. A woman lies on the floor looking panicked. It's OK – she knows help is on the way. Surely we're not there yet?

Both let you know, in hushed tones, about the other's stupidity or infirmity, as if to prove their own superior fitness or mental state. Your father couldn't remember where his brother lived this morning. Your mother's having trouble getting up the stairs, you know. You want to point out that it's not a competition – no one's winning here. There are check-ups and blood tests. Prostates and prolapses. Aspirin and Warfarin. Minor procedures. Major ones.

And one day, as you're brushing a child's hair with one hand and holding the phone away from your ear with the other, you realize that the dynamics have changed. It's you calling them to see how they're getting on, popping in to see if they need anything. It's you helping them make sense of things – usually the energy bills. You're picking them up and dropping them off – not at parties, but hospitals and funerals. It's hard, but you've finally accepted that you shouldn't take the ironing round any more or get them to drive for three hours to babysit. The truth is, they've become a bit of a worry.

And you feel guilty because you've leaned on them so much, and expected such a lot from them. And the bolshie teenager in you – the one that still lurks there under the expensive face cream and workwear – she feels a bit sorry for herself, too. A bit pissed off with them for getting so bloody old while you weren't watching. You haven't had a chance to relax yet. And now you have all this extra stuff to deal with, they're another thing, on top of everything else. Welcome to the sandwich generation.

But mostly you feel a bit sad because you know you're short on time. Will they be here for the next birthday, the next Christmas? And it dawns on you that they must have gone through the same thing with their parents. Felt as exhausted and uncertain. This is some genuine Circle of Life shit happening, right here. And you want to thank them for everything they did. But it's all a bit emotional, really. And far too cheesy to say out loud.

M.I.A.: Your Career

Spunking all your money on childcare

One of the great shocks of parenthood is just how much childcare costs. It shouldn't be a surprise, because it's something you've heard friends bang on about for years. But when they told you how much they were paying, and how little it meant they brought home each month, you secretly thought they were exaggerating or sending their child to a nursery made of diamonds or something. It couldn't *really* cost that much, could it? Because how would people do it?

Then the time comes for you to start investigating childcare, and it becomes clear that your friends were telling you no word of a lie. Childcare is *expensive*. If you keep your old office job, with its massive commute and culture of presenteeism, it is crippling. If you jack that in and follow your dream of doing something family friendly from home, there will be no way of paying for it at all.

And when it comes to childcare, there is a bewildering array of options out there. The upscale choice is a nanny, but there are hidden costs involved with this, the first being tax. Plus they'll need to fill their days somehow, which means that, on top of their salary, you'll end up resentfully paying out for soft play and snacks. Also, there's a strong chance that your child will start referring loudly to his nanny in public, making the rest of the world think he is an overprivileged little tosser.

Nurseries aren't exactly a bargain option, but at least they don't call in sick or spend the afternoon on the phone to their boyfriend in New Zealand. But they, too, have their downsides. Send your child to nursery at a young age and people have a nasty tendency to go all judgey on you. You can expect lots of pointed 'admiration' from friends and in-laws ('I'm so impressed you can do that. It must be so difficult'). You may find yourself responding with defensive comments about what a fabulous environment it is, and how much your child has learned. Even though she doesn't appear to know much beyond how to make you feel monstrously guilty when you say goodbye.

And good luck getting them in. When you laughed at all those mothers signing up their babies at birth, it turns out you really were supposed to do that, because these places have waiting lists longer than the Nile. If you're not type-A organized about it, you will end up at your second, third or even fourth-choice nursery. Admittedly, this is no big deal in the scheme of things – they all have the same garish toys and weird, poo-cum-cabbage smell – but it will be one more thing to beat yourself up about.

The third option is a childminder. This has its advantages – your child will likely have playmates; it's often cheaper – but again it leaves you reliant on one person, who may or may not be a psychopath the second the door is closed. And, as with a nanny, it can be awkward when it turns out your child hates their guts.

Whichever option you choose, it will eat a vast chunk of your salary each month. Certainly it doesn't surprise you when you read that childcare costs more than the average mortgage. You wonder what the hell it was you spent money on before you had this hulking great outgoing. Clearly you wasted the opportunity, anyway. You could have cultivated a healthy Louis Vuitton habit or travelled the world staying at the Four Seasons.

You try not to resent your friends with willing and able grandparents, the ones bitching like mad that their mother plies the kids with sweets and then acts surprised when they don't eat their dinner. Yes, you want to hiss, but THEY DO THAT FOR FREE. It may reach the point where you quit your job because the numbers simply don't add up. Either way, you find yourself counting the days until your child starts school, when you can start staying at the Four Seasons. Or not.

Finding your vocation

One of the great perks of motherhood is that it gives you the excuse to jump ship on that job you always hated. After all, you didn't have a baby so you could leave him from 7 a.m. to 7 p.m. with some homesick Romanian teenager you found on Gumtree. Not when it's going to eat up 90 per cent of your salary, anyway. Yeah, you're out of there, suckers. Or you will be just as soon as you've got your second maternity leave.

Quitting your job isn't short on benefits – one of them being that you get to look down on those mothers who continue with their careers, as you cook up elaborate meals in the mornings and make tight-lipped comments about 'priorities'.

There is a downside, though: after eight months spent scouring gloomy church-hall playgroups for potential friends, singing 'Wind the Bobbin Up' at a baby more interested in eating the pushchair wheel, you'll have had just about enough. At home you'll have all the status of a slave; at parties everyone will tell you you're doing 'the most important job in the world' while clearly thinking the opposite.

All of which may leave you looking for a new, post-baby career. Ideally this will be something reasonably stress-free you can do between the hours of 10 a.m. and 2.30 p.m. Which basically leaves dinner lady. The other option is to become your own boss.

The good news is that this won't seem as daunting as it once might have done because all those hours spent sitting in parks/John Lewis's fourth-floor cafe will have given you plenty of time to think of ideas for new ventures – all aimed squarely at you. Why, you rant at similarly frustrated mothers, has no one thought to open a pub? But not just any old pub – no! One with a playroom attached! Complete with babysitters! Or a nail bar – with a playroom attached! Complete with babysitters! Sadly, these plans usually fizzle to nothing after ten minutes spent contemplating the realities of running a pub-cum-crèche. But no matter – there are other choices available to you . . .

Such as mum fantasy-occupation #2 – the holiday let. The appeal here lies mostly in dreaming about owning a massive house in the countryside (or France, if you're feeling adventurous), where you will magnanimously let people stay for money. It's a good fantasy occupation this, allowing you to overlook all the horrible cleaning-and-admin-type work involved in running a B&B, and instead concentrate on the fun bits, such as whether to paint the bathroom floorboards black or white. It doesn't matter if you can't afford the big house, either. Thanks to endless hype about glamping, it's enough to buy a knackered caravan on eBay and stick it in the garden, strung up with bunting and fairy lights.

Failing that, you can use this opportunity to fulfil any long-held creative ambitions. Babies sleep for, what, fifteen hours a day? Which surely gives you all the time you need to write that novel/create that multi-screened video installation you always wanted to. Unless, that is, you need to earn actual money. In which case, there's always selling things. In the old days, this might have meant schlepping around your neighbours' houses hawking Tupperware or make-up. But not any more. Because, thanks to the internet, you can now sell all sorts of tat. And not just any old tat, either. You can sell *tat you've made yourself*. Cushions, greetings cards, hand-stitched felt slippers – the world is your ropey market stall.

Indeed, you may well find that your new, alternative career is based around monetizing a hobby, such as selling cakes or ceramics. This is partly because it lets you work from home and set your own hours. But it's also because your options are more limited than they would have been thirty years ago. Whereas at this juncture your mother's generation might have gone back to university or retrained, that isn't really a goer now that doing so costs as much as a house in Portugal.

Which is why so many mothers are embracing the start-up culture. Running your own business is more accessible than it's ever been. Set up your own restaurant and, well, that's going to cost money. Selling beef jerky from the back of a camper van or starting a ceviche pop-up in a disused railway arch – not so much. And it's lucky for us that jobs like running a market stall or food van, which might once have been considered boring or menial, are now chichi and lifestyle. Once upon a time, your average market stallholder looked like Pete Beale. Now it's all women in sixties-style eyeliner and Anthropologie aprons flogging salted caramel brownies.

As well as having fashion on your side, there are other benefits: friends and family will congratulate you on how enterprising you are. If you're really lucky, you'll appear in a patronizing *Daily Mail* feature about mumpreneurs. Though quietly terrifying, it's the opportunity to chase your dreams and do something new and adventurous. Plus, being a self-run, set-your-own-hours type of affair, it means you have time to go to the gym *and* get to tell people at parties you do something interesting.

There is a downside, which is that it's insanely hard to make a hobby pay. Even Sophie Dahl struggled to shift her cookbooks. Often people think your cakes/cushions/cards are fabulous, but never get round to actually buying them. You work out your hourly rate and discover that you make less than your sixteen-year-old babysitter. And she gets to watch iPlayer and raid your treat drawer all night. After that, it's only a matter of time before you decide that making cushions/greetings cards/hand-stitched felt slippers is kind of an arse-ache. There's also a surprising amount of admin involved. After the fifteenth hour spent queuing at the post office, you may find yourself yearning for that job you always hated.

Grannies as childminders: Learning that there's no such thing as a free lunch

It's the dream scenario, surely? While you go out to work, your mother/mother-in-law looks after the kids. You get to earn a wage and actually keep it; the kids are with someone who genuinely loves them – everybody's happy.

OK, so maybe now that you think about it, there are a couple of niggles. It's fine that your mother/mother-in-law wants to be adored – you totally get that. And yes, you know that grannies are supposed to stuff their grandchildren with biscuits and God knows what other crap. But does it *have* to be after snacktime? And when you happen to mention that maybe, just maybe, she could give him water instead of juice, does she really need to do that tight-lipped thing that implies you're being neurotic and mad, when she only has to pick up a newspaper to know that fruit juice contains more sugar than a Krispy Kreme and is a direct road to obesity, diabetes and heart disease? And that's without even mentioning what it does to their teeth.

And while you wouldn't dream of dictating what they do with their day – you appreciate, after all, that she's doing this for free – it would be nice if she didn't stick them in front of the telly for *quite* so long. Yes, she's got her heart condition to think about, you totally understand that. But would it kill her to come up with some creative play around the table, rather than immediately falling back on CBeebies? It's not like you expect her to take them to the Science Museum every day or anything, but the odd trip to the local farm or adventure playground wouldn't go amiss. God knows you've dropped enough hints, leaving out leaflets and offering to let her know the websites of interesting places to go.

And yes, now that you mention it, you have a couple of issues with her timekeeping. If a nanny rocks up late, she'll at least take the trouble to think of a reasonable excuse. She won't say, 'I was going past John Lewis on the bus and thought, "You know what, I need a black cardigan," so I got off and went to pick one up.' A nanny won't call you thirty minutes after she was due to arrive and say, 'I'm in Morrisons, do you want anything?' when you *specifically told her* you were on a deadline and can buy your own milk, thanks all the same.

Now that Granny spends so much time at your house, she sees how everything works (or rather, doesn't) and likes to chip in with her own ideas. 'Can I make a suggestion . . .?' she says, eyeing the stash of unopened mail on your countertop. Or, 'You know I don't like to interfere, but . . .' before proceeding to interfere. You try not to let your irritation show, but she can probably tell from your tone that you're not best pleased with her.

Not that she can talk – the woman is the queen of passive aggression. She washes up everything that isn't chained down, and pointedly asks if you've got any rubber gloves, when she knows you didn't the last time she came and won't the next time, either. 'Have you thought about hanging your laundry out, rather than putting it in the dryer?' she says, like it's the first time she's thought to ask. If she wants to have a dig at you, meanwhile, she does it through the baby: 'Yes, Mummy's made that chilli *very* spicy, hasn't she?'

The truth is, you get what you pay for. Say what you like about a nanny, but she'll understand that what you want is help, not an opinion. She won't act like the fount of all knowledge when it comes to anything child-related, unlike Granny, who had hers thirty-odd years ago and can scarcely remember what happened last week. She won't tut every time your kids act up, and imply that it's your fault for not disciplining them properly. She won't make snarky comments about you going out to work in the first place. Honest to God, you just can't get the staff.

Obsessing about other women's work/life balance

As the mother of young children, you might not get the chance to *do* much, but while you're freezing your arse off at the swings, you do have lots of time to think about stuff. And one of the many things you may find yourself spending too much time dwelling on is other women's work/life balance. Meet another mother of preschoolers and you're instantly curious to know: How many kids has she got? Does she work? If so, how many days a week? Are her children with a nanny? A nursery? What are the logistics of her life?

You immediately compare this with your own situation and, if it is in any way different, judge her for it. 'I just couldn't do it,' the full-time working mother and stay-at-home mum say of each other, like they're not both crippled with jealousy that the other gets to have uninterrupted conversations with real, live adults/hang out in coffee shops during the day.

Whenever you get a moment to read the paper, you inevitably find yourself drawn to the articles about 'having it all', even though there are dozens of them, every day, and you must have read everything there possibly is to say on the subject. Are working mothers neglectful? A good influence? A bit knackered and doing the best they can? You know every angle of the arguments, but can't resist checking to see if the author has found a fresh take and given you something else to feel bad about. In the same way, your ears prick up as you hear another *Woman's Hour* presenter talking about childcare policies or fawning over a female CEO and begging to know how she does it (easy: she pays other people to).

What's depressing is that you still even have to think about this stuff. You thought the whole point of being born post-1970 was that other women had done all the protests and sit-ins, and you could just sweep in with your blow-dry and power suit and take over the world, like the heroines of the Jackie Collins novels you grew up on. Except about the only woman to have done this seems to be Tamara Mellon.

If you came of age in the 1980s or 1990s, you probably grew up assuming you would have it all. Chances are you didn't even question the idea. Sure, your mother's generation might have been stuck doing the heavy lifting at home and fitting in crap, part-time jobs around school hours. But that wasn't going to be your life – God, no. Yet a straw poll of your university friends reveals that most have taken a backseat to their partner's careers, either jacking in work completely or doing something flexible and low stress (i.e. boring and badly paid).

Naturally there are the high-flyers among you, the Sheryl Sandbergs and Amal Clooneys of your little friendship group. But they've never got time to see anyone, and so bear the brunt of everybody's snideness. Woe betide them if they confide that they missed their child's birthday or took an extended work trip somewhere far-flung. On the rare occasions that you do get to catch up with them, they make you feel mumsy, with their Chanel lipstick and screw-you handbags. These are the women who get to the gym at 6.30 a.m., 'because it's the only way I can fit it in'. Hmph, you think piously, they must hardly see their children during the week at all. Because adopting a superior attitude makes you feel better about your own choices, in the way that looking at Angelina Jolie's veiny arms on the Sidebar of Shame makes you feel better knowing that beautiful people are flawed too. Although the joke is the idea that you actually had a choice, when childcare costs a billion pounds, or you moved out to an area where there are ten jobs, nine of which are on a farm.

And because most jobs these days involve gruelling hours, plus an hour's commute at either end, you feel that you and your partner can't both do that, unless the kids are never going to see a parent at all. And since one of you has to think about the birthdays, doctor's appointments, swimming lessons, shoe fittings, PE kits, after-school clubs and other commitments that seem trivial and easy until you actually have to deal with them, and discover that they eat whole days and don't leave much headspace for actual, like, job stuff . . . you end up stepping back and feeling like Betty Draper, only with scraggy hair and a shit, part-time job.

And you realize, to your surprise, that for all the campaigning, the books, the ranting, the fights, the *decades* of all-round effort, nothing much has changed at all.

On the Home Front

Failing at the domestics

You didn't like to say it out loud – lest you compromise the feisty anti-housework stance you'd maintained till now – but you were secretly quite excited about maternity leave. Not only because of the lovely baby you'd be having, but because it meant you'd finally get to play at all that domestic stuff.

As a busy working girl, your repertoire extended to wrenching the wet clothes out of the washing machine and trying not to drop any socks as you transferred them to the tumble dryer and rammed the door shut with your backside. You only ever ironed clothes if they'd been on the floor more than one night. You cooked, yes, but were no stranger to a Waitrose chicken saag if you were hung-over or home late from the job you used to have – the one where you wore nice clothes and had drinks with live males after work, and generally swanned around looking fabulous while holding pieces of paper.

What you were really looking forward to, now you were going to be a mother, was batch-cooking – whatever that was – and putting things in freezer bags like a proper eighties mum. You were going to hang your wet clothes on an actual line and get a nice retro peg bag and saunter around the garden with a basket on your hip. You couldn't wait to fill your (imaginary) larder with mysterious store-cupboard essentials like bouillon and bouquet garni, and yeast for all the bread you were going to bake. Kirstie All-sopp, eat your heart-shaped muffin out.

Why you should look forward to this sort of thing is unclear. Maybe millennia of oppression conditioned you or maybe a double dose of X-chromosomes really does make women better at wiping surfaces. Either way, you felt that running the home was a rite of passage on your journey to complete womanhood.

And then it starts. Laundry on an epic scale. Mountains of clothes – yours, the baby's, your partner's – all stuck together with sick and blood and milk and poo. It's never clear whose. You ask your mum how you can get them clean – surely you can't put poo in the washing machine? She tells you the joke about how you're supposed to soak them in a bucket of detergent! Ha ha ha! Then what are you supposed to do with them? Anyway, you don't have time for that – the mountain is growing, like a sinister blob from a fifties B-movie.

Sometimes babygros full of baby shit fester at the bot-tom of the laundry basket. By the time you get to them, they're so grim you just quietly throw them away. Order-ing six more packs of impossibly cheap babygros online, you try not to think about the ethical and environmental impact of your inability to soak shitty clothes in buckets, and feel like a failure as a woman.

Your thoughts may turn to your great-grandmother, who had thirty-three children, including eight sets of twins, and only a mangle and an outside lav. And you may wonder how they did it in those days, and feel like even more of a failure. Later, as you glance at the hieroglyphics on the care label for your one nice jumper, you may ask yourself what those symbols mean (*Hmmm, a triangle inside a square?*). You shove it in anyway and hope for the best, only to pull it out and find it has shrunk to the size of the babygros. And it occurs to you that this domestic stuff is hard work actually, and you are failing at it quite spectacularly.

Your plans to do a Delia and get with your freezer don't come to much, either. You try freezing a few stews and chillies and whatnot. But freezing stuff, you discover, also means remembering to get it out of the freezer the night before. Naturally you refuse to get a microwave because of the cancer-rays, even though that one appliance would probably transform your life. Another fail.

So you end up with a freezer full of indiscernible brown dishes in bags and ice-cube trays of weaning gak (nice one, Annabel Karmel), which you eventually throw away because you aren't sure how long you're supposed to keep things in the freezer. And can you defrost them and reheat them without getting salmonella?

You've discovered those baby-food pouches now, anyway, and it becomes your guiltiest of pleasures to sit the baby in the car seat on the kitchen table and let him suck the pureed mulch through the plastic nozzle like a little astronaut while you get on with your jobs. Anything to avoid fishing cutlery out of the dishwasher. What is that big flashing S on the dishwasher for, by the way? Somebody said you had to put salt in it, but that's a joke, right?

As the months pass, the washing never sees daylight,

and you come round to the idea of fish fingers as an acceptable midweek supper for all the family. And you curse your education for not teaching you about home management and laundry-care labels. Then you remind yourself that you don't want to do this shit anyway, and have a proper career out there somewhere. And you rage at how the system sets women up to fail at work and at home. You get yourself in quite a massive tizz about it for a moment, until the sound of the washing machine finishing its cycle brings you round, and off you go again.

Coming to terms with the plastic

No matter how non-judgemental you fancy you are, there was probably at least one occasion, pre-kids, when you went round to the house of a breeder friend and thought the following:

1. Fucking hell, that looks like hard work.
2. If/when I become a parent, I will never let all that Fireman Sam/Disney Princess crap through my door. What are they thinking, giving house room to that tat? My poor eyes are bleeding. Don't they know it's landfill waiting to happen? It's like they don't even *care* about working conditions in China. All I can say is that if/when I have children, they will be allowed a Sophie giraffe, a Melissa & Doug sushi set and one of those ride-on wooden ladybird things. And that's it. You won't see my parquet eclipsed by the contents of the Argos catalogue. No, thank *you*.

Then you have children and start coming across brands like Djeco and Le Toy Van. Mmmm, yes, you think, French brands. Or at least brands that sound French. They're my style. You pick up some tastefully muted garage on the hunt for a price, and are aghast. '*How much?* So not only am I expected to spend my hard-earned on breast pads and bath thermometers, I'm now supposed to drop fifty quid on some stupid garage?'

So you don't end up with quite the number of stylish wooden toys that you thought you might. You take a rain check on the Vilac ride-on classic car and the Moulin Roty teepee. In any case, you read somewhere that Scandinavian children have far fewer toys than British kids and are much happier for it. He can play with a saucepan and some onions, you think. That's all they want at his age.

Meanwhile, your friends act like they're doing you a major favour by passing their own crap down to you, sabotaging your no-plastic policy but making you look like a prat if you say as much. You consider dumping it all on the nearest charity shop, but some small kernel of your sorry, pretentious soul feels guilty for being a no-fun, dates-are-the-same-as-toffees-honest kind of parent.

Or, more likely, your kid catches sight of that broken Buzz Lightyear and loves it 17,000 times more than he ever liked the £28 wooden bus you succumbed to, which by this point has been smashed into pieces that somehow never stick together again, even though the superglue won't come off your fingers.

For a while, you try to stick to your guns, mentally categorizing toys as either 'good' or 'bad'. Some fall into a grey area, such as vintage Fisher-Price (it's plastic, which is bad, but old, which is good!). Ditto Lego, which is good if it's the sturdy, primary-coloured blocks of your youth, but you're not sure about this nasty, flimsy modern Lego, and the way what kids build is preordained. This snobbery dictates what you buy for other children, and as you choose yet another birthday present, you wonder, shall I buy this for the parents or the child? The parents generally win, and the child fails to hide his disappointment as he unwraps something an Edwardian might have played with.

But there comes a time when you can resist the tide of plastic no longer. And once you give up, it's liberating. It's surprising how quickly you get used to the plastic. And somehow the Peppa Pig My First Sit-and-Ride, in its shade of weather-beaten Pepto-Bismol, doesn't jar as much as it did when first you allowed it into the garden. And now it's here, the IKEA tent and pop-up tunnel might as well join it. And what harm the kiddie skittles set or the bucket and spade?

Because, suddenly, everything you hated about plastic (its indestructability, that it's made so cheaply) becomes exactly what you love about it. And that helicopter – the one with the flashing lights and whirring propellers – might be annoying, but it keeps him busy in a way that the tasteful-looking farmyard scenario never does. And, frankly, if it gives you five minutes to blow-dry your hair, it can stay.

Soon, when child-free friends come round, you spot that flicker of surprise as they clock the Postman Pat van with the missing door or the Barbie & Me Glamtastic Hair Style Book and Salon Playset. And you want to make some sort of apology or at least acknowledge that you know it's tacky and vile, and ecologically unsound to boot. But, by that stage, you really can't be bothered.

Knowing all the Farrow & Ball colours

Unless you're very posh and get to inherit all your furniture, there will likely come a time when you have to buy your own. Admittedly, this isn't without perks. Buying home furnishings is a rite of passage, a sign that you're becoming a grown up. No more mattresses on the floor for you – you're getting a real bed! No more throws to hide rank landlord armchairs – you're buying your own sofa, baby!

But when you've never bought furniture before, it's hard to know where to start. Clothes are easy: you've had a lifetime buying those, and have made enough mistakes to know roughly what you like and can afford. Furniture though? That's a different ball game.

It usually starts with you being sniffy about IKEA and instead going to all the trendy shops you've heard of – the Heal's, Conran Shops and SCPs of this world – before seeing the prices and having a minor coronary. Seven hundred pounds for a laundry basket? How is that even possible?

You exit these places, with maybe a bowl or a mug if you're feeling profligate. Then you try the antiques shops. But these seem just as expensive and smell funny too. Plus they're filled with their own idiosyncratic stock, only ever made up of things you're not looking for.

So you go crawling back to IKEA, telling yourself you'll jazz up whatever you buy with some great cushions or something. But even at the cheapest shops furniture is never exactly a giveaway, so there's a huge pressure not to get it wrong. And when you don't know your own tastes, this is a minefield. Is that pink sofa jaunty and fun, or just camp? Are those Eames chairs a classic or a cliché? It takes a certain confidence, and a lifetime spent reading interiors mags, to really know.

Similarly, it's a rare person who doesn't care what anyone else thinks. Will your friends look at that pineapple lamp stand and think it's cool or utterly naff? Will those neon wall lights, so cutting edge now, date within the hour? It's no wonder that, when it comes to decorating, you're incapable of making a decision.

So when a brand like Farrow & Ball comes along, there's a reason you pounce on it. Received wisdom tells you that F&B is the last word in good taste. Yes, it's more expensive than all the other paints, but compared to those laundry baskets, it's the bargain of the century. And given how pricey houses are these days, it's not like you'll have a big area to cover, right?

The bonus of Farrow & Ball is that someone else has gone through and weeded out all the old-lady lilacs and tacky golds. So it doesn't really matter what colour you go for, it will still pass the taste test. With another paint chart, you buy what you think is a lovely shade of cream only to realize too late that it's magnolia. With F&B it will be called something like Tallow or Pointing and will radiate quiet sophistication, or at least tell the world that you paid a lot of money for your paint.

The downside of this is that everybody else knows it too, so when you go round to friends' houses, you will endlessly spot those familiar shades of grey and taupe. You'll see them in cafes, restaurants, pubs and shops – everywhere you go, in fact. If you live in an up-and-coming area, you'll notice that the Farrow & Ball-painted front door is a visual shorthand for 'Yes, I've done my house up', a way of differentiating it from the crack den next door.

Soon the colours are so familiar you find yourself playing spot the shade. 'Ah yes, Down Pipe,' you say. 'We did the boys' bedroom in that.' And it dawns on you that your fear of getting it wrong has turned you into a type, one that comedians mock on panel shows. Because the sad truth is that, without you even noticing, your tastes have become dull and conventional. You are one of the herd. So you tell yourself that you've got to branch out and embrace a different brand of paint. But which one, you wonder, is considered acceptable?

Not knowing what to do with your garden

How does your garden grow? If you've literally no clue, read on.

Nothing says 'grown up' like having a garden – one that isn't open to the public and full of playground equipment (i.e. a park). For everyone knows that an outdoor space attached to your very own house, ideally with rhododendrons in the borders and a rockery full of alpines, is where Family Life happens. It's where the memories are made.

You know, the halcyon days of your youth. With the water fights and the barbecues and the kids from next door.

You have to get a garden, and the bigger the better. 'Has it got a big garden?' is the first question your parents ask, every time you tell them about the latest house you can't afford (that you are hoping they will give you the deposit for). Old people are obsessed with you having a garden. The implication presumably being that the size of your garden is in proportion to your child's well-being and future happiness. No garden? You have failed. Your child will get rickets and Social Services will take them away because all they do is watch *Roary* and eat Quavers in their playpen.

And damn it if you don't actually agree with them for once. Man, you want a garden. Oh, hold on, what you really want is 'outdoor living'. You want a rusty French-looking dining table and chairs, with a big floppy parasol and coloured tea lights and warm-white festoon lighting. You want storm jars and citronella candles, cashmere wraps draped idly over chairs. You want good friends sitting around, enjoying your effortless hospitality: tables groaning under the weight of your vibrant summer eats, mozzarella and torn basil everywhere, people choking on sprigs of fresh mint and lavender and whatever else Sarah Raven says will taste nice in a Bellini, honest. You want to Cox & Cox the living shit out of that garden.

And then you get a garden. And you literally have no clue what to do with it.

This fact may not dawn on you straight away, however. If you are lucky enough to have the spends, you may merrily proceed with accessorizing your 'outdoor living room' and assume this means you are 'doing the garden'. Taking delivery of your decorative metal chickens and Provence plant stand, you will feel like a proper, sophisticated grown up and invite some of the guys over to partake of your laid-back outdoor lifestyle. You'll spend a day in IKEA stocking up on solar-powered lighting (which, no one ever seems to acknowledge, simply doesn't work), scatter cushions and large plastic jugs in zingy citrus shades for all the coolers you'll be serving. You'll spend a month's wages on tea lights and candles to ward off mosquitoes, even though you live in the Midlands and there haven't been any mosquitoes since the drought of '75. You'll paint every surface French grey and spend whole weekends constructing log stores and erecting off-white sail shades, so they can rot in the rain over the summer.

If you are especially enthusiastic, you may set up a compost bin run entirely by worms, which – you tell your horrified father – only cost £150, and you can use the special compost 'tea' to feed the plants in the garden.

Oh, yes. The plants. You knew there was something you'd forgotten. This patio titivating is all very well, but lurking there at the edge is a lawn that needs mowing, and around the lawn there are borders that need . . . bordering? Some gardens have ponds (um . . .?) and trees with real fruit on, that falls off and lands all over the floor like organic Lego. What are you supposed to do with all those damsons? Can you even eat damsons?

If you're lucky, your parents might come by and help out occasionally. Your dad will mow the lawn and get those stripes like you had in the seventies. Your mum will spend hours pulling out dandelions (all that ever came of the wildflower seed bomb you chucked over the grass) and planting bulbs, which she explains may or may not come up next spring. NEXT SPRING? What's the point in that? You don't say this out loud, but instead head inside to finish your online shop at Cox & Cox because there's 20 per cent off on some Fiesta string lights.

Later on, they will talk to you about top soil, and blood and bone, and how next-door's laburnum will need cutting back as they can be poisonous, and have you been to the car-boot sale, because you can get seedlings there from a man who does five nasturtiums for a pound? And Linda from over the road said she will give you some of her irises which are perennials and that's what you need, something you don't have to worry about that comes back every year.

You smile and nod and give them big hugs and say thanks ever so much. And, closing the door, you acknowledge that you have literally no clue what they are talking about, and that this gardening stuff is really quite a bore. And you wonder exactly where and when you are supposed to garner all this gardening knowledge. Your experience as a child amounted to little more than growing a sunflower and having your own watering can with a spout in the shape of a daisy. And you wish for a moment that you hadn't always thrown away the gardening section in the paper, that over the years their cryptic headlines like 'Time to divide your primroses' had come to mean something to you. You think of all the Sundays you spent in beer gardens, when you should have been in garden centres.

You feel disappointed, too, by your partner, who

seems even less savvy than you about this stuff. And your unreconstructed-feminist-self wonders what the point of him actually is, seeing as he can't put up shelves or knock through the kitchen, either. I mean, the guy doesn't even own a spade.

Occasionally you spend some time in the garden, trying to manicure this unwieldy, unfamiliar territory. But your heart's not in it. Because, frankly, dead-heading the clematis is at the bottom of the list, after more pressing tasks like raising the children, feeding the family, earning half the money and doing the everything else just to survive. And you realize that this is why only old, retired people have nice gardens – because they've got nothing else to do.

Buying a big telly

Middle-class people don't, as a rule, like big tellies. Owning a titchy TV, ideally with a fuzzy picture you have to squint at to make out, shows your priorities lie with more cerebral things, like reading metaphysical poetry. It's all part and parcel of that British thing of wanting to make your house as uncomfortable as possible. There is a weird prestige in this – to the point that, at the very top of the social strata, people live in freezing homes with threadbare rugs and buckets of water to catch the rain.

Indeed, anything that might be deemed comfortable – thick, shag-pile carpets, generously stuffed sofas, a fridge that you don't have to unpack to know what's in it, is considered vulgar. And a massive, plasma-screen telly, with its

Benefits Britain connotations and implicit suggestion that you might actually watch your TV, is most vulgar of all, up there with Saddam Hussein's paintings of big-titted blondes watching warriors fight giant snakes.

Your average visitor from Mars might be forgiven for thinking that the television is a fairly innocuous piece of household technology. But there are a million unspoken rules. Your TV can't be too big; it can't be in the bedroom. If it's going to be wall-mounted, it shouldn't be above the fireplace. If you have an 18-inch cathode ray from 1986 – or, better still, no TV at all – then kudos to you. (Although, in the words of Joey from *Friends*: 'You don't own a TV? What's all your furniture pointed at?')

The dream is to join the no-telly brigade, where the prize is getting to tell everyone how your children make puppets and perform self-penned plays instead of cabbaging in front of *Tiny Pop*. And they're *so* much happier for it. 'Honestly, you can't believe how much more creative and resourceful it's made them.' The prize, in other words, is getting to make other parents feel bad.

But even if you're nicer than that, a part of you may still feel uncomfortable with the notion of having a giant telly – you know, one of those 52-inch jobs that immediately commands your attention when you walk into a room. These aren't TVs that you can tuck away in a corner or hide in a cabinet. They tend to dominate. It's hard to find somewhere to put them except, y'know, the middle of the wall. And this makes the TV the focal point of the room, suggesting that you value it over framed souvenir posters from long-gone exhibitions.

But once you have kids, you have a more pressing

reason to buy a decent telly. Because the maths on going to the cinema doesn't work any more (when you're looking at £25 for two tickets and £30 for a babysitter, before you've even chucked in drinks, popcorn and travel, it had better be a bloody good film).Which means that, if you're going to see anything made post-*Avatar*, you're going to have to watch it at home.

And watching movies on an 18-inch cathode ray really isn't the same, even if it does stop you spending five quid on a giant cup of watered-down Sprite. There's a reason they invented HD and surround sound. It's better. So as a mother you can find yourself torn between your desire to have a decent viewing experience and your longing to look clever, a dilemma only made tougher by the fact that big TVs are so cheap now. (£199 for a 40-inch LED TV! They're practically paying you to have one.)

Either way, these are issues you may find yourself thinking about more now that you're a mother, because you are, by definition, a homebody. Once it didn't matter that your flat looked like a monk's bedchamber, because you were never in it. You would no more have spent a weekend 'sorting the house' than you'd have spent it going to the airport to watch the planes. But these days you've more incentive to file your credit-card statements and paint that damp patch on the wall, because you're confronted with them all the time. Come Monday, when people ask what you did at the weekend, you're embarrassed to tell them the truth, which is that you spent a good two hours clearing out that drawer full of crap in the kitchen – *and found it really satisfying* – so you find yourself muttering something non-committal, like 'not much'. And that's where you're going wrong. Because if you had a giant telly, you'd be more inclined to watch quality box sets, which would at least give you something to talk about.

Regretting the dog

A year or two after you've finished childbearing (although research shows that the fever can take hold earlier in those who've never been to the countryside or cared for an animal in their lives), you wake up one day and decide that your life is simply not difficult enough any more. You need some fresh hell, and must get a dog.

It's not clear why so many of us experience this impulse. Perhaps it's because we are so used to living with small creatures who cannot control their bowels and like to slobber over everything. Once our own offspring have learned to use the toilet and stopped gnawing the furniture, there's a big, wet, poo-shaped hole in our lives. And since for most of us another child would mean moving house, getting a bigger car and, oh, having sex, the dog seems the most sensible option.

Yes, you actually tell yourself it's the sensible option. Of course you've heard the stuff about how hard it is to own a dog, blah de blah de blah. You know you can't leave them on their own all day, don't you? And you can't take them on holiday. And they cost almost as much as that third child, but with none of the future ROI. They smell, shed their hair, shit all over the garden. The bitches bleed around the house and the dogs get so excited whenever anyone comes to visit, they jizz on the sofa. You do know this, don't you?

But it's pointless trying to tell you anything by this stage. You've bought a one-way ticket to Dogsville. Puppytown, here you come. 'Think of the benefits!' you tell your mother, who quietly points out you're already struggling to cope with the demands of your life, and perhaps a dog and the responsibility that comes with it might not be what you need right now. Yeah, whatever, Grandma. Think of the benefits! The children will learn all about taking care of animals and stuff. And everyone knows that kids who live with dogs don't get asthma and allergies. And they'll have to walk it, so they won't get obese. You are basically doing this for the children's health. You say this with a withering glance that implies she should have done more for you as a child, and that, thanks to her, you probably have only months to live. So you're going to get a dog and it's all her fault.

It will give you a reason to get out and walk every day, you tell her. You're going to get so into walking. And they've invented dogs that don't smell or shed their hair nowadays, so the cream carpet in the lounge will be fine. Lots of people have dogs, so I mean, how hard can it be? And she'll look after it when you go away, won't she? You don't even hear her answer as you're already Googling dog neckerchiefs and wondering whether to get the full-length Hunters or those short ones that are a bit like pixie boots. But do they shorten the leg?

Six months later and your kids have just run dog shit through the kitchen and up the stairs. There is toxic *merde de chien* all over their new school shoes and their friend definitely has some in his hair. Your husband promised he'd pick up the doggy-do from the garden, seeing as how you've already dealt with so much human crap – including his – over the past few years. But he never seems to do it. Funny that. And so the garden has become a poo-minefield. The children have to run a gauntlet of the stuff to get to the trampoline at the bottom, which the dog is now spinning around on, fully believing she is one of the children.

Briefly you marvel at the energy of the hound, before remembering guiltily that she hasn't been walked today. Or yesterday. It's impossible to find the time, you justify to the imaginary RSPCA inspector, who is taking photos of your mangy skeletal dog, standing forlornly in your imaginary yard, to use as evidence. The truth is, the dog is a bit fat. You just find it so boring walking her round and round, and she makes such a mess in the car afterwards, and you can't ever get the mud out of her fur. Plus you don't like ambling along holding a bag of shit. So you sometimes 'accidentally' forget to bring the poo bags, and spend the whole walk pretending to be engrossed in bird song or taking a really important call from the President, while the dog curls one out in the middle of the footpath. It seems that no one in your family wants to pick the stuff up.

In a fit of rage about the poo-garden situation, and fully premenstrual – as you now seem to be for at least twenty-eight days of every month – you decide to overlook the fact that you never walk the dog, and that it was you who wanted the bloody thing in the first place. You resolve to teach your partner a lesson about leaving dog-logs on the lawn. Gathering the smelly socks he scatters around the house like woollen elephant droppings, you place one on each mound of shit, firmly pressing them in to achieve an artful, cherry-on-top look that you admit would not be displeasing under different circumstances.

And it is most pleasing to you when he gets home and sees what you have done. You get a great deal of enjoyment from watching him in silhouette against the sunset, gagging as he tries to salvage his socks. It's like that scene in *Gone with the Wind* when Atlanta burns, you think, only without the kissing and Clark Gable. It's less enjoyable when your friend drops by, unannounced, and wonders with a squint what your husband is doing out there in the garden. Is he . . .? Are those . . .?

And you realize that you have lost your mind, and your mother was right all along. You should never have got a dog.

Feeling obliged to enjoy baking

One of the many activities mothers are under pressure to like is baking. We're constantly reminded of its inextricable link with hearth and home. Food is an expression of love, people say (always the ones who are good at cooking, you notice). So it's embarrassing to admit that you are bad in the kitchen, or bought your child a SpongeBob cake at Asda, rather than handcrafting a circus scene, complete with big top and ringmaster. It implies you are at the very least slack, and at the worst, cold and remote – a sort of anti-Nigella, if you like. Baking is the hallmark of a proper mum, one who can fashion toys from pipe cleaners and doesn't forget to pick her kids up from nursery.

Every so often you have a go at baking because you feel you should, rather than through any burning desire to make banana bread. But it is messy and faffy. The ingredients are expensive, especially if you are being fashionable and replacing all the fun bits with brown rice syrup and almonds. Often it doesn't turn out that well. They'd have done a better job at Greggs.

You may struggle with the idea of being an old-fashioned wife, stuck in the kitchen. You don't see your partner whipping up a red velvet cake of a Saturday, and nor would anyone expect him to. Having said that, you don't necessarily have a problem with the notion of reclaiming feminine crafts. You can see the tongue-in-cheek appeal of a frilly pinny. And you certainly aren't averse to a butterscotch blondie. But the trouble with reclaiming feminine crafts is that it's not like something else gets dropped from the list to make up for it. So if you take up baking, you don't get to ditch the laundry or the dog-walking. It just becomes another thing on the list.

And is it just you or is this whole baking schtick ever so slightly competitive? When a mother plonks a fresh-from-the-oven carrot cake on the table, there's a sense of one-upmanship. Baking is a look-at-me skill. Most mothers can't bake because they know they'll be as fat as houses within a fortnight. So it becomes an activity for thin, perfectionist women, who do it on top of their careers and children, to show you what fabulous all-rounders they are.

Fair enough, though, it isn't all about showing off. A good part of it is about creating memories. You want your kids to look back with fondness at Mum's ginger molasses cake and see it as a dish no one can ever replicate. Although give them a bag of M&Ms often enough and they'd probably attach the same emotional significance to that. In any case, there are no guarantees. You could spend half your life making your special cookies only for them to admit on your deathbed that they always found them a bit sickly.

The compromise is to keep baking as an occasional thing – something to do on high days and holidays. The trouble with this is that, if you only bake occasionally, you probably won't be very good at it. And once you've invested the time and effort in those coconut macaroons, it's annoying when they turn out like fossilized remains. Not least because you can't understand it – you followed *all the bloody instructions.*

And so you come to understand why there's such a market for those posh little bakeries, the ones selling apricot and almond-polenta muffins at £3.80 a pop. Because as overpriced and silly as they are, at least they get you out of doing it yourself.

Habits Old and Bad

*Smoking and being sick in the taxi –
reliving your misspent youth*

By the time you give birth, you've been behaving yourself for what feels like for ever. You may have abstained totally from alcohol during pregnancy; you may have had the odd glass at dinner parties, if you're not American. A glass is acceptable over here, although it must be accompanied by the speech about how all the research says that it's fine to drink in moderation, but the NHS needs to cover itself. At this point someone may mention French women, who allegedly neck red wine throughout pregnancy and are told by their doctors to cut back to five cigarettes a day. You all then get to roll your eyes at those crazy French, before agreeing that you, with your lone glass of Prosecco, are the very picture of temperance.

Having this conversation on repeat is a high price to pay for one glass of wine, so you may find you don't even bother. And having been on the wagon for so long, you look forward to falling back off it once the baby's born. But it turns out to be more complicated than that. The conundrum then becomes how much you're allowed to drink while breastfeeding (answer: always one glass more than you've actually had). Experienced mothers tell you to 'pump and dump', because they like the way the phrase trips off the tongue, but at this stage you're still baffled by the bottles and tubes and which bit goes where, and it's all a bit daunting.

Anyhow, a part of you is embracing your new wholesome life. Look at you, up with the lark without a hangover! You wheel the buggy around the park on Sunday morning, noticing with a combination of smugness and alarm that you're the only person who hasn't been there all night. In the Costcutter queue, you're the only woman not doing the walk of shame. Ha, you think. They must feel even worse than you do.

But as nice as it is to feel superior to other people, the trouble with your new wholesome life is that *it's just so wholesome*. Yes, you are now the Ella's Kitchen demographic, but you don't want to be *only* that person. You want to be handed the flyer for the cool new club night, even if you don't actually want to go. In other words, you are torn between your old life and your new one.

If this is your first child, you have the added pressure of showing that you are totally taking this baby business in your stride. Having bitched like mad about those friends who have babies only to disappear off the scene for three years, you are acutely aware that you need to show face on a night out sometime soon. Which, in any case, you bloody deserve.

So you go out, pleased to get into your pre-baby clothes, even if that does involve two pairs of Spanx and the lie that those jeans never did up properly anyway. You trowel on so much Touche Éclat you look like you've just returned from a week in Val d'Isère circa 1988. You feel dismayed by your rack, which, despite being a 36FF, looks less Christina Hendricks and more your old headmistress.

But, for a few hours at least, it's lovely to kid yourself that you are something other than a nurturing moo-cow. Until 10.30 p.m., when you will start to fret about the babysitter, you are your old, carefree self – someone who belongs in pubs and bars. No one here would even know you were a mother. Three glasses in and, eager to test that theory, you start harassing young barmen, saying things like, 'You'd never guess I was thirty-eight and had two kids, would you? WOULD YOU??'

But your brain, always slow on the uptake, hasn't clocked that your body can't do it any more. You drink like you used to, but can no longer handle it. For a full year after giving birth, you are the drunkest person at weddings, the one dancing when nobody else is and flirting boorishly with whoever drew the short straw of being seated next to you.

If you can get past the knackeredness, that is. Because the reality is that most of your chat ends with you staring dead-eyed into space, before coming to and saying, 'Sorry, what was I on about again?' With the clock ticking, you need to pack as much of a big night out as you can into the three-hour window available. Because you desperately want to feel naughty, but haven't got the recovery period to be *really* naughty, you sneak outside for a cigarette, even though you haven't smoked in years.

And it's the cigarettes you blame when you end up vomiting all over the bathroom, like some fifteen-year-old who's been guzzling the Mad Dog 20/20. Those and your tolerance levels, which you now remember are through the floor. 'I only had, what, three glasses of wine? Hardly anything,' you tell friends the next day. Except they beg to differ, reminding you that they could scarcely prise the bottle from your grip.

This kind of behaviour has a shelf life, however, because looking after a baby on a hangover is a circle of hell even Dante didn't dare imagine. Within months you are making up prior commitments, and hoping friends bail on nights out so that you don't have to. Quietly, but surely, you are preparing to disappear for three years.

Admitting you are alcohol dependent

If you get drunk at home and nobody is there to see it, are you even drunk? This is the sort of searching philosophical question you may ask yourself as you put away that bottle of Romanian Pinot Noir your friends brought over last weekend, which you thought was a bit cheapo at the time, but turns out is quite nice actually. And you should really buy more Romanian wine, because whatsit who knows about wine says Eastern Europe is the new New World of wine. Oh dear, it's all gone.

Text to partner returning home late from work: *GET WINE.*

It depends on how old you were when you had kids, and the kind of lifestyle you led beforehand, but chances are you didn't do a lot of drinking on your own at home before you got pregnant. The 'solo lash', as your male friends sometimes referred to it, was the preserve of, well, your male friends. They, like their fathers before them, possessed the casual confidence to drink by themselves and not think anything of it. But, crucially, they always did it in the pub, with a newspaper and the din of Sky Sports as their foil. In the same room as other people. In a convivial atmosphere. The general aim being to share a spot of bonhomie in the company of other bon hommes.

As a young professional woman, your alcohol-based play was also usually a public affair, but always with friends. Friends and wine, wine and friends, some Marlboro Lights, some nineties food piled high on a big white plate and drizzled with something or other, more wine. You never saw your drinking as a problem because everyone did it, and they did it together. Drinks after work, Monday to Thursday. Massive night Friday, obvs. Clubbing or a party Saturday nights. Sunday lunches that never ended. Oh, what larks.

Then along came baby and it was time to get the bill and neck some metaphorical Berocca. Let's be honest, by that time you were grateful for the detox. And you surprised yourself by how much you enjoyed this enforced sobriety. On social occasions when pregnant, you watched with a tight-lipped gaze, somewhere between boredom and horror, as your friends guffawed proudly at their own jokes and repeated them until closing time. 'I'm totally not drinking again once I've had the baby,' you'd think to yourself as you went to the loo for the eighth time, because it was genuinely more interesting sitting on the toilet than around the table with that bunch of pissheads.

Then you had the baby and, without even noticing you were doing it, you began to enjoy a medicinal glass or two in the evenings. This was usually administered by your husband, who had realized early on that this was something he could do without being told off. At this stage you couldn't actually drink any more than that if you tried, seeing as how you had to go to bed at 8.30 p.m. if you were to have any chance of achieving four consecutive hours' sleep.

But it became important to you, this little reward for your efforts. You might not be necking Prosecco with the laydeez in snazzy West End restos any more, you would rationalize, but you could achieve your own small high right here at home, without having to get the polenta out of your hair. It's a little piece of the old you, you would tell yourself. Something they can't take away. Some light relief after the day's hard labours. A way to switch off. And some other stuff about antioxidants and that island in Greece where they all live to a hundred and drink wine all the time.

Initially you begin to take this little pill at teatime (oh, OK, let's just say it: wine o'clock), a glass to take the edge off while you wrestle the small one into the seat that isn't securely attached to the table, and shout at the big one, who is spitting on the polenta, apoplectic because you switched off *Chuggington*. Moving upstairs, you top yourself up because, well, bath time is a dangerous mix of tedious and stressful, and the edges must be further softened if everyone is going to get out of the bathroom alive. Meanwhile, Daddy's sending you texts, protesting that he's having a terrible time at work, when we all know he's just eking out his day, deliberately missing trains and pretending to be important so he doesn't have to get involved in bath time. He thinks he can waltz in the door like some fucking superhero and give them a kiss just as they are going to sleep. The wanker.

As they get older and you begin to push your own bed-time back a bit, the wine continues to flow throughout the evenings, because it's nice to enjoy a glass or two with lovely Daddy once he's actually home, and it's much tidier to finish a bottle anyway. That's right, you are basically tidying up by having that extra glass. It's so true what they say: a woman's work is never done.

Occasionally Daddy may be away for work. Or maybe you and Daddy have split up, after you found out he lost his job last month and has been spending all the money drinking and online gambling. However it is that you come to be alone at home with the kids of an evening, you notice one day that you are polishing off this big bot-tle of Romanian Pinot Noir, not because you are especially stressed (they ate all their dinner and got themselves ready for bed. In fact, they've gone to bed, when did they do that?) and obviously not because it's sociable. Not unless you count stalking your ex on Facebook as socializing.

Nope, you are pouring yourself another big glass of this truly excellent Romanian Pinot Noir because you really, really like it and you cannot cope with the thought of what it would be like *not* to have its velvety finish glid-ing over your tonsils right now. Mmmm, this Romanian wine really is very nice. And as you tidy up that naughty messy bottle, you start to feel quite philosophical about life, and ask yourself: if you get drunk at home and nobody is there to see it, are you actually even drunk?

Becoming a baby bore on social media

The internet has taught us plenty over the years, such as how to apply liquid eyeliner, and never to let a boyfriend photograph you naked. But some lessons have been harder to learn. Facebook, for instance, has been around for more than a decade, but when it comes to using it properly, it still feels like we're feeling our way in the dark, making enormous twats of ourselves in the process.

Because it's so easy to get it wrong. You'd think the rules would be simple enough. Don't brag. Remember that 96 per cent of your Facebook friends only know you a bit and, far from being delighted if you go on holiday, actively hate you for it. Don't share inspirational quotes or recipes for vegan, gluten-free cakes; the world will collectively roll its eyes at you.

Of course, it's easy to be sneery about social media and to tell everyone that you're never on it these days. The above-it-all stance may be the cool one to adopt, but it's infinitely harder to pull off once you have a baby. Then you are suckered. Because dicking about online is about as social as you get these days. Facebook and Instagram's hours are as irregular as yours are. They give you something to look at when you're pushing a swing, heating up beans or doing some other mildly depressing activity you need distracting from. Have the social-media sites on your phone and they fast become a habit, a way of checking in with the world without actually having to speak to it.

Because you're on Facebook a lot these days, you have more opportunities to get irritated with the other people on it. A few are entertaining – namely the ones who use it as a forum to share their jokes or mental breakdowns. But for the most part people behave appallingly on social media, in a way you'd like to think they never would in real life. They bang on tiresomely about their pet bugbears, whether that's the SNP, animal rights or how much better New York was back in the day. They make you look at their holiday photos, which until about 2001 everybody knew made you the dullest person alive. They are shamelessly needy, posting photos of themselves that say, 'Look, everybody, I'm hot!!' These serve their purpose, making you feel both unattractive and depressed, but backfire when you next cross paths with that person and they've aged a decade.

But all those years spent lurking on Facebook pre-children have taught you something. You know that acquaintances have no interest in your baby photos, and that to them one two-year-old looks the same as all the others. In any case, when looking at your pictures they're far too busy judging your furniture to pay attention to your offspring. You get that it's mean to post photos where you look good and your friend looks a mess. You know not to post shots of yourself on the beach, at a party, in a flash car, or anything else that makes you look like a shit, middle-aged version of those Rich Kids of Instagram.

You know all those rules. And then you break them. Because, while you don't want to drop your friend in it, it's so rare you look nice these days the world needs to see it. And look at you! Finally on a beach, after a year of being up to your elbows in turds! Better post that one, too. And here you are, drunk with the old gang. Hilarious – everyone will love that pic. Maybe not the people you forgot to invite, but hey ho.

Then there are the photos you post because everybody else does, so you assume you can get away with them: your child's first day at school, World Book Day, their birthdays, nativities, seeing Father Christmas. The trouble is that there are a lot of these occasions, so your baseline posting level is already high enough to bore everybody you know into a coma. Add to that the holidays, day trips and times you just thought they looked cute, and you're that scene in *Airplane!* where the other passengers start killing themselves rather than listen to any more of Ted's stories.

You know all this, and yet you persist, because your child is pretty, goddammit. The world just needs one more picture so that they can see it, too.

Marathons, triathlons and other midlife crises

They're always there, cluttering your Facebook feed. The grinning, sweaty faces showing off the medal they've picked up for their latest marathon, or badgering you for cash because they've decided to cycle to Belgium for Macmillan.

Maybe I should do something like that, you think. I mean, it sounds awful, but they look so . . . happy. How can they be so thrilled? They've just run twenty-six miles. But the pride and satisfaction in their eyes makes you feel like you're missing out on something – a big secret no one's let you in on. You notice that, like fried chicken and bad boyfriends, marathons seem to be addictive. Only at least they come with the bonus of leaving you in great shape. A healthy addiction – hmmm, how do you go about falling into one of those?

What you need is a goal, you decide. Maybe if you signed up for some race or other, you'd have the impetus to start running every night. After all, once you'd made the commitment, you'd have to do it, wouldn't you?

But you quickly realize that you can't go running every night because you have 85,000 other things to do, and by the time you've finished those tasks, you no more feel like running than you feel like working night shifts in a cheesecake factory. Early mornings aren't an option either because if you got up any earlier you might as well not bother going to bed.

And which punishing activity to choose? There are so many now: the marathon, Tough Mudder, that one where you get to run 268 miles across the Pennines in January. There is no end of new and gruelling experiences on offer. In fact, there seems to be a whole industry devoted to putting you through hell. And their marketing is good. You have the nagging feeling that, like bungee jumping, and going to the cinema on your own, an extreme fitness challenge is something you should try once in your life.

And you'd like to be able to boast about having done one. You could casually drop your time into conversations, post those sweaty-but-elated pics on Facebook, feel smug about doing your bit for charity. Better still, doing it once would give you the reassurance that you *could* do it. In other words, you can't be that clapped out because you ran a marathon. It would basically give you the excuse you need never to do any more physical activity, ever again.

But one circuit of your local park is enough to tell you that you're not cut out for a marathon. How can they do it? Twenty-six miles of this? But it's so boring. You forgot to make a proper playlist and now you're stuck listening to the *Desert Island Discs* podcast, and it's one of those lofty types who disapprove of anything written after 1863.

And, looking around you, everyone else looks so much better prepared for this. How do they manage to travel so minimally? Meanwhile you've got your cash card, keys and iPhone stuffed into your sports bra, along with poo bags for the dog and an emergency tenner. It's like the Rocky Mountains in there, only sweatier.

The back of your throat hurts. It's so hard to breathe properly. Surely you should stop and walk for a bit now? Ah, that's better. In any case, you definitely read that interval training is more effective than flat-out exercise. And that's what you're doing now, isn't it? Walking, with a bit of jogging thrown in. Yes, that's more like it. Much better for you in the long term.

But it feels a bit lame to be walking, especially given how many runners are now jostling past you. In fact, the volume of traffic along this towpath is enough to tell you that running has become quite the thing. Although you already knew that, what with all those blogs and apps you keep seeing, and those running leggings with Aztec patterns all over them.

It's not just the younger lot either – a good chunk of this crowd is made up of women like you. Your friends, once gym-shirkers to a woman, now feel no shame in inviting you to Pilates or suggesting the odd game of tennis. You're so active, you mothers these days. You don't think you saw your own mum ever break a sweat. Her idea of a workout was walking around House of Fraser.

But now it's all military-style boot camps and extreme spinning. In the eighties, exercise – if you did it at all – was to a video, often watched while eating ice cream. Along with Callanetics, the big fad was toning tables, your experience of which could be summed up as 'lying down'. But women were more gentle on themselves back then. Mums were allowed to get away with looking like mums. You didn't have a fifty-one-year-old Elle Macpherson Instagramming pictures of herself hanging off yachts in a bikini, making us all feel inadequate.

But much as you'd like to look nice in a bikini, on a yacht, a marathon starts to feel optimistic, given your other commitments. Maybe a 5K around your local park is more realistic. Or perhaps a Zumba class. I mean, all that running is just going to knacker your knees, isn't it? And you hear of people actually dying on these things. That's got to defeat the object, surely?

No, the more you think about marathons, the more they seem like a bad idea. Your poor nipples have been through enough without all that chafing, and you don't even want to think about what it does to your toenails. Could you live a happy and fulfilling life without ever having run a marathon or done an Iron Man? You suspect that you could.

Not Knowing Where to Live

Thinking about moving to the countryside

If you're a parent in London, you will at some point have thought about moving to the country. Even if you're a committed urbanite who secretly thinks the world beyond Ealing is a there-be-dragons place full of in-breds and racists, you will at some point have thought about it.

Because how could you not? The countryside is sold to you as a better upbringing for children. It gives them a *Swallows and Amazons*-style experience, one where they can roam free, exploring riverbanks and learning mysterious skills like bushcraft and foraging. In the country they won't be mugged for their iPhone or stabbed for their bike. You won't find them playing with 'crystals' that turn out to be broken glass. They will have the innocence that comes with not living down the road from a brothel or knowing a crackhead from a smackhead.

But forget the kids, what about you? You could have a house with wisteria and roses, and those raised flower beds like Jamie Oliver has in his house. You could have an actual lawn and spare rooms. You look on Rightmove when you should be sleeping, and know for a fact that for the price of your poky hovel you could get a mansion with turrets and a guest house, and what's more it would cost you three hundred pounds a month.

OK, so you'd spend the difference on train fares and petrol. And since you don't hunt, shoot or fish, and only really walk as a means to an end, you're not 100 per cent sure what you'd do with yourself. But while the country lifestyle doesn't in itself appeal, the accoutrements do. There's a part of you that could fancy an Aga and a tongue-and-groove kitchen. You could have a wood burner and a wicker basket filled with logs. You see flint cottages in newspaper property sections and mentally redecorate them so they look like Babington House.

And while it's great having all these amazing bars and restaurants on your doorstep, when did you last go to any of them? Do you really want to be in your forties and still hanging out with the twenty-five-year-olds? Yes, you spraff on about culture, but when did you last go to an exhibition or play, if you're being honest? Does an annual trip to the Tate really warrant a £3k-a-month mortgage? Besides, London is for young professionals. You want to live somewhere geared to families, where you don't feel like a weirdo for carrying a baby instead of a Michael Kors bag and a copy of *Stylist* magazine. In any case, you'll only be an hour or so away – hardly more than your current commute, when you think about it.

The countryside would free you from the city's shallow distractions, allowing you to get on with writing that novel or starting that business. Blood sports might be out, but you could have proper hobbies, like gardening or horse riding. You could drive everywhere without having an anxiety attack about parking, and humour the locals when they complain about the traffic.

Yes, they might hate you and call you a DFL (Down From London) behind your back, but find a southern town these days that isn't full of DFLs. And for you this is the great thing. It means that the pubs have already been gastroed and the cafes will serve the Americanos and overpriced spelt muffins you feel at home with. Choose the right place and it will hardly be a culture shock at all.

It also means you can avoid that whole bunfight over schools – no lying about your address or faking a religion necessary. You can simply send the kids to the local village primary where there will be twenty pupils in the year, all with the kind of pushy, keener parents who join the PTA and fundraise so that you don't have to. You imagine the parties you could have, in your palace. You could have friends to stay for the weekend, where you cooked elaborate lunches and drank red wine all day. That's what you should be doing at your age, not hanging out in style bars pretending to be twenty-three.

Admittedly, you're a bit stumped when it comes to which part of the countryside you'd move to. The Home Counties are the obvious choice, being commutable, even if real country people do sneeringly call them suburbia. But you are not a real country person, and while you're all for fresh air and views, you don't necessarily want the full experience of being snowed in, surrounded by sheep carcasses.

It would be lovely to escape the crowds and distractions of the city, though, you think. A rural life would have more meaning. It would take you away from London's grasping materialism, and the way it has of making you feel shit because you can't spend £200 on some sunglasses.

But you are nervous – nervous about moving somewhere new and hating it. You like the fact that you can walk to M&S and that the corner shop stays open all night. You have friends here, even if they are all slowly drifting out of town. OK, so you might not go to the Tate that much, but you could if you wanted to, and that's the point, right?

Yet still you have doubts. So when friends move to the country, you track their progress avidly. 'How is it?' you ask. They are invariably positive, talking about the space, the quality of life, the close community. They tell you how happy they are, and how surprised they are not to miss London more. 'They hate it,' you tell your partner on the way home. 'I could tell. Sure, it's great to have that big house, and the garden and the trampoline. And the garage would be useful. But I could see she was dreading us leaving – she's so lonely during the week. How could you not be? No, it looks nice and everything, but I just couldn't do it.'

You then spend two hours queuing on the Westway, and finally arrive home to find two empty beer cans and some vomit on your doorstep. Which is when you start thinking about it all over again.

Trying to persuade your friends to move to the countryside

If you've been styling it out with kids in London or some other critical urban mass for too long, moving to the country can feel not unlike waking up in paradise.

Whether you relocate to the countryside proper – as in down a lane, with fields and the smell of shit – or to somewhere slightly less urban, like Warwick, it can be hard for the city dweller to acclimatize at first. When you're used to having the buggy stolen from outside your flat, it's impossible to believe how free and easy life can be here. People leave real eggs from real chickens' butts outside their house for you to take, and you're supposed to just leave the money in an honesty box? That is mental.

Once you've settled into your new reality, and the kids are in the teensy-tiny school and you've been to the fête and pressed cider with the Village Idiots (that's what they call themselves, they're mad!), you start to think about making some friends. You like everyone here – it's great to connect with people who aren't defined by their careers or material worth. And you chat with people of all ages. You never talked much to anyone in their eighties before you moved here. I mean, really talked to them. Passing the time of day with the folk in the post office is something you've never done before. And it's so handy that they slice breaded ham right next to the till. They have pretty much everything you need in there.

Yep, life is kind of perfect here in paradise. Everyone

should totally live here. In fact, why don't they? Wouldn't it be so great if some of your old mates lived here too? That would be the icing on the Country Slice. You miss those guys. You picture them, there in the city, drudging around, all grey and full of respiratory disease, and feel so sorry for them. Pity the children! What kind of a life is it, when you can't run free among the shit and buy sliced ham at the post office?

If only you could persuade them that life would be better here, with you. Then you'd have the best of both: urbane friends, with all their wit and style, right here in the country, with all its fresh air and animals. And you could still do all the other things you used to do together in the city, like getting drunk, but do it in the country. In pubs with horse brasses round the fire, where Wednesday night is Meat Night. It's just so funny, here in the country.

So you decide to show them what they're missing. And a great PR campaign is born.

You invite them down to stay. Show them a good time. Kind of like a press junket to your life. You take them for a long walk, showcasing the very best the countryside has to offer – past the thatched cottage where they can see an honesty box in action and get some of those sprouts on a stick as a souvenir – bet they've never seen them before. The walk ends in a cosy village pub, where the guest ale has a hilariously rude name like Badger's Cock, and you all get obnoxiously drunk and piss off the locals with your loud hysterics about badgers and cocks. Everyone has a jolly time and says things like 'it's so great to be out of London' a lot. After a casual Sunday roast (organic pork from the local farm – it's almost gamey, so different when it's outdoor-reared) you drop them at the station and recycle a quantity of wine bottles the likes of which your village has never seen.

They come again, this time with the kids. Now's your chance to sell them a lifestyle. Give them a taste of your local honey. You make sure the kids don't bath for two days beforehand, so they can look properly free-range. Then you force your guests to follow you as you pretend to go about your usual rustic Saturday. Your look is country-fabulous: Hunters, the cashmere with the holes in and a slept-in ponytail, basket in hand. You pop in at the butcher's (Britain's oldest family butchers, this) and swing by the farm shop so the kids can see a real goat and you can buy some muddy vegetables. Lingering at the estate-agent's window, you point out the five-bedroom pile with the wisteria they could live in for the price of their one-bed maisonette on the Roman Road. It's a great place to stand as everyone you know is in town this morning. (They always are, it's not exactly somewhere you can disappear in.) This makes you look exceptionally popular. Look at you, waving and chatting to all the quirky locals as they pass by.

Then it's down to the beach for another walk – OK, so that's pretty much all there is to do. Still, it gives you a chance to dazzle them with your list of all the famous people who live here. Yeah, Martin Clunes is in the next village and we see Fiona Phillips in Waitrose *a lot*. Did you know we have a Waitrose now?

You list the times the area has been on telly. Did you ever see that BBC2 version of *Persuasion*? The bit where she falls over? That's filmed just over there. And the guy who wrote *Harbour Lights* with Nick Berry? He used to live in that house. Walk for long enough and you can also get in how the schools are tiny, not mentioning how it means they mix up the years, so the school is really just one massive class. And throw some stuff at them about reconnecting with the landscape and being close to nature. Which is how we humans are supposed to live, after all.

They start to show a few buying signals. Result! What are the job opportunities like? As far as you know there is being a farmer or working in the new Lidl – the one you and the other incomers fought so hard to oppose. You're only here because your parents retired nearby and you need the free childcare; your husband works away. So you spin a line about how living in the country encourages entrepreneurialism. You have to create your own jobs; everyone here is so creative. And now there's the internet, you can do anything really. 'What like?' they wonder. Um, anything! Oh, look, is that an eagle?

They ask more questions. 'What do you do for fun?' Well, life is less about meaningless socializing these days. We're enjoying being more active – doing a lot of walking. 'Have you made any good friends? What are they like?' We're connecting with all sorts of people – have you ever really talked to an eighty-year-old before? 'What do you do for shopping?' We're trying to be less wasteful. We do everything online – it's much greener, and the nearest city is only an hour away if we need it. But we find we don't want as much. Life is less materialistic here. 'What's the transport like? Does it take long to get to London?' I am sure that's an eagle.

Waving them off, you wonder if you sounded a little

sanctimonious, or else plain dull. But you stop worrying when you get home and spend the evening on Facebook, posting pics of your ruddy-cheeked children playing with the dog and looking super-healthy in various wide-open spaces. You never let the pictures show the monster, petrol-guzzling car, packed with shopping from Lidl, that you have to go everywhere in because there is no public transport.

And the people come and go, and they always love getting out of London, and you send them links to all the bargain fixer-uppers and B&Bs-for-sale that come up on Rightmove. But eventually the weekends tail off. Your campaign loses momentum. Is it that you stop inviting them? You've realized it's not much fun having guests with three under-fives who trash the place. Or is it that they stop wanting to come? 'When is she going to stop trying to make us move to the godforsaken country? We only go to get out of London for a bit. And she's only there for the free childcare. Why does she keep banging on about Waitrose? Everywhere's got a sodding Waitrose.'

And eventually you give up trying to persuade your friends to move to the country. You've made some new friends now, anyway. They're really nice. They've just moved down from London.

Moving to the countryside and realizing you made a terrible error

For the first year you love it. Here you are in a place that people pay to go to on their holidays, and yet you actually live here. In fact, an extended vacation is exactly what it feels like. See how beautiful it all is. Just look at those ancient churches, the manor houses and mills. Where are the Chicken Cottages, the Poundstretchers, the Cash Converters? There are no sirens or crime-scene barriers or crazy ladies shouting about Jesus. The local postcards are not photographs of shit-looking shopfronts hilariously labelled 'Welcome to London', but actual picturesque views. Everything is just so *nice*. It feels like you've rocked up in Toytown, if Toytown had a Crew Clothing Co. and a boutique hotel.

As an arriviste, you take a keen interest in the local area and its past, relaying your town's albeit humble claims to fame to everyone who visits. Look, there's the house that Anne Boleyn once visited. Did you know that a famous opera singer lives three villages along? Yes, the town has a fascinating history of rope-making.

You visit the local petting farms and laugh at how vastly superior they are to their London equivalents, where an out-of-place donkey chews on some shipped-in hay overlooking the railway track. You buy meat and milk direct from the farm, even though it's both expensive and kind of gross. Having never given much thought to the homogenization process, you secretly miss it. You are forced to wise up to the realities of country life, where you coo over the lambs in March, only to notice they disappear without trace nine weeks later. You notice that the lowing cattle sound exactly like the opening bars of 'Meat is Murder', and feel a bit weird about the whole hunting thing.

Still, you embrace the cider festivals and the fêtes and the country shows, and tell yourself that this was what London really lacked – a cohesive community where everyone got together, regardless of age or background. You chuckle at the headlines on the local-newspaper hoardings and congratulate yourself on living in a place where someone driving into a lamp post makes the front page. The other day you left the back door open and no one robbed your house. As if that would happen in London! Can you imagine?

You become unwittingly smug, baking crumbles with the apples from your garden and filling vases with the flowers that grow like weeds outside. And to think you used to spend £10 on a bouquet from Columbia Road, or worse, Kenyan roses that exploit poor farmworkers and drain the earth's resources. In fact, you don't consume nearly as much here. You do things on a Saturday afternoon that aren't traipsing around shops. You have old-fashioned Sundays, with a walk and a proper lunch.

You remark on the changing of the seasons, which truly comes as a revelation. It's something you can smell in the air and see in the changing colours and light. There is beauty in all of it, whether it's the frozen leaves crunching under your boots or the low hum of bees in summer. You're sure that it's true what they say – there is no such thing as bad weather, only inappropriate clothing, so you buy outerwear from those twee chains on the high street you swore you'd never frequent.

But you have to adapt your wardrobe, because here your city clothes make you look like some kind of angry crow. Besides, your shoes can't cope with the mud. And the noise! People are always moaning about the city being lairy, but no one told you that every morning the birds would go on a mission to drive you insane. Similarly, the dark nights take some getting used to – where are the street lights? And power cuts are a novelty. Though the Wi-Fi is just annoying.

A few months later you realize that there is such a thing as bad weather, and in this country we are cursed with it. Why is it always raining? And what are you supposed to do with yourself now? You can't face going for another walk because the landscape is always the same. And there are only so many routes you can go on because, for all that talk of freedom and space, most of the countryside is actually owned by someone, usually an arsehole farmer who shouts at your children if they stray on to his fields.

You look out at those fields, the ones that initially struck you as so beautiful, and wish someone would build a Westfield on them. You start to miss the museums, galleries and other indoor places you could take the kids. Here there is the leisure centre and a soft-play venue on an industrial estate. Neither reflect the rural idyll you were sold. Yes, there are playgroups and activities, but these take place on the third Thursday of the month at 9.30 a.m. and you lack the organizational skills needed to keep track of them.

The stately homes and places of interest that you visited so keenly in the early days are expensive and don't stand up to repeat trips. You're not that interested in walled gardens, if you're honest, and there are only so many tea rooms you can visit in a year. On nice days these places are crowded and tiring, and on cold ones they are empty and bleak. You miss the South Bank.

To make yourself feel better, you tot up the money that you haven't spent – on flowers, on fripperies, on going out. You no longer waste money on takeaways because it's like 1986 out there, with just an Indian, a Chinese and a chip shop to choose between. Nor do you spend money in bars or restaurants because the high street becomes a ghost town after 5 p.m. There are some great pubs, sure, but these aren't much fun if you have to drive. The cafes are pleasant and laid-back, but the restaurants are mostly Sunday-best places, full of geriatrics in sports jackets tucking into the table d'hôte in silence. You miss sushi and pho. You miss Ethiopian food, even though you never ate Ethiopian food.

True, you could still go out in London, but getting there is too much of a shag. That hour-long journey you were promised doesn't quite pan out once you take into account driving to the station, delays and the fact that you aren't actually going to Victoria. And it's a journey you've come to loathe, with its uncomfortable seats and relent-less strip lighting. The night train is horrible, packed with drunks eating Burger Kings and missing their stops. This is even more annoying when it's you.

You miss things that you didn't expect to miss, like the barrage of posters advertising musicals, albums and exhibitions. Because without these you quickly lose touch with what's going on and become that person who looks blank every time someone mentions a film that isn't *Frozen*. You miss the Botox wives, the fashion students and the Middle-Eastern tourists on spending missions because at least they gave you something to look at. You miss being able to say 'London' in a tone that says 'trump that, loser' when people ask where you're from.

Increasingly, you find yourself asking questions: Why is

everything closed all the time? Why is everybody so old? Why is there nothing to do on a Sunday except have sodding lunch? You contemplate moving back, but know this would mean trading in your house, with its lawn and apple trees, for a two-bedroom grot-hole on the A40.

So you remind yourself that your village, with its friendly people and wholesome vibe, is actually pretty nice. You remember how lovely it is not to deal with the filth and the traffic, and the idiots in the crowd. And you tell yourself that this way you get the best of both worlds, since you can always visit London when the kids are a bit older.

Because what else are you going to do?

Holidays and Other Misnomers

Pretending to enjoy camping

Growing up, the best holidays were always the ones spent in some Spanish resort, where the food came in a plastic basket and the ice creams were rendered as frozen lemons. Your parents ignored you and you had the time of your life doing colouring competitions, while they got drunk on sangria and had affairs.

How times have changed. In the same way that the Nazis at NCT convinced you it would be better if childbirth really hurt, so their chums over at Camping HQ tricked you into believing that sleeping in your clothes and eating only sausages for a week is somehow better than getting a tan and drinking cocktails from a pineapple.

Camping is basically a big, cruel joke played on women who believe they are going on holiday. At the heart of this sick charade is the seminal text, *The Cool Camping Guide*. This clever work of fiction – let's call it *Mein Campf* – has duped millions of us into booking camping holidays in the UK, instead of going to some generic sunshine island where the drinks arrive in the aforementioned pineapple.

It's from this very tome that you may find yourself booking somewhere smug in Dorset, where the site facilities include recycling and a compost toilet. You wanted glamping but your husband – who as a boy once slept in his friend's garden, but has re-imagined his childhood as that of Mowgli from *The Jungle Book* – insists it's not really camping if you have a proper bed. So you go the whole hog and book an eco-friendly place where the children's activities are listed as collecting the eggs and petting the donkey. As you approach the site in a damp sea mist, unwashed children emerging from the woods like zombies, you feel a pang of nostalgia for your sun-drenched kids' club and lemon ice-cream holidays. But by then it's too late.

Because, despite the Cool Camping propaganda, for mothers camping isn't actually about foraging for mushrooms and toasting Fairtrade marshmallows. It's about packing and unpacking things, sometimes for up to a week before and after your trip. During any given camping experience, your packing schedule includes, but is not limited to:

- plastic tubs full of healthy snacks no one will eat
- plastic tubs containing mackerel fillets you've been marinating like off *River Cottage*, but look too rancid to cook once you arrive
- bags of clean clothes
- bags of dirty clothes
- waterproof clothes in case it rains (it will)
- summer clothes in case it is hot (doubtful, sorry)
- warm clothes for the evenings
- the kids' entire collection of pyjamas, some weed in

- washing-up bowls full of dirty plates
- washing-up bowls full of clean plates
- ice boxes full of freezer blocks that don't keep anything cold
- jute bags bursting at the seams with Aigle wellies, Birkenstocks and Crocs

But the fun doesn't end at packing. For mothers, camping is also a chance to experience all the status anxiety of being at home, but in the great outdoors. Because no matter how much Cath Kidston bunting and solar-powered fairy lights you bring, you will always end up camping next to someone in a bell tent who brought a chimenea and their fucking guitar, and is probably wearing a flower garland in her hair, aged forty-three.

Your other half does not, as he implied he would, become all rugged and outdoorsy either. Despite his claims to be Bear Grylls, the fresh air and those tiny bottles of beer he's chugging on all day seem to render him horizontal most of the time, and definitely not rubbing sticks together and building bivouacs with the kids like he said he would.

At some point you may slope off to do the washing-up. Standing there at the sink with one cold tap that you have to hold down to get anything out of, you can finally lose yourself in the peace and quiet for long enough to switch off. And as you stack the washing-up bowl up for the fifth time this weekend, in your Boden 'happy' pull-ons, the truth dawns on you that the highlight of your holiday has been washing-up one-handed in cold water.

That's not what you tell your friends when you get back, of course. As far as they're concerned, you really enjoyed the kids being 'free-range' and 'going feral' and it was so great because they didn't look at a screen once (although secretly you made them watch *Cars 2* on the iPad, three times).

Next time, when the talk turns to summer holidays and camping, you can't help Googling 'holidays in Spain with kids' clubs'.

Not knowing where to go on holiday

Let's say that you are fortunate enough to find yourself with both the time and money to go on holiday. Perhaps the stars have aligned so that you can afford to go somewhere *in the school holidays* that isn't Wales. Whoopee! Hooray! Next comes the question: where the hell do you go?

Camping in France sounds like a solid choice – that's what everybody did when you were at school. It's always popular, not too flashy, and you can tell yourself it's educational because the kids will likely be learning French at some point. You know where you are with France, but it's big enough that there's always somewhere you haven't been before.

But when you start Googling French campsites, it becomes clear that this isn't entirely what you had in mind. Where are the teepees, the Airstreams and the tree houses? You thought they'd got rid of all that depressing green nylon, and that these days it was all sheepskin rugs and Moroccan pouffes. This looks suspiciously like actual camping, with sweaty tents lined up in rows and nowhere to put your clothes.

You mentally hoick your budget and upgrade to something you don't have to erect yourself. It feels pricey now. But even so, something is lacking. You weren't expecting a fortnight at the George V, but it's a mobile home in a holiday park. The website photos are probably the best it will ever look, and the website photos look like that place in Great Yarmouth where your gran used to take you.

You wonder what they've got over on Airbnb. Ah, this is more like it. Here are some places that look promising, in fancy-sounding destinations. OK, so maybe the wallpaper's a little eccentric in this one. And that rocky, cliff drop of a garden doesn't look too toddler-friendly. You're not sure about being on the fifth floor without a lift, either.

Oh, but look! Here's an apartment complex deep in the Tuscan Hills with charming, rustic decor and a shared infinity pool. And it's surprisingly affordable – way more so than a hotel. Jerome from Brisbane says that 'tranquillity is guaranteed – the only sound you'll hear is the birds and frogs'. It looks idyllic. And at that price, a complete bargain. You start picturing sunset carafes of Chianti, wild boar ravioli, the odd day trip to Florence.

Your partner bursts your bubble by asking, 'But what are the kids going to do?' Immediately you draw a blank. They will enjoy the views and the sound of silence. You imagine your two-year-old throwing a fit because you opened his yoghurt for him, destroying Jerome's tranquillity. You flash-forward to yourself, shushing small children while everyone else around the pool quietly wills you to die. It's no good. Tasteful apartment in the Tuscan Hills isn't going to work for you. Besides, with a rural apartment complex it's just the four of you. No babysitting, no entertainment. Nothing but you and the scenery.

So you decide to go the other way. You're thinking kids' clubs and waterparks, somewhere they can meet other children and bust some moves at the mini-disco. Maybe Eurocamp or some package deal. But these are surprisingly expensive – that price is *per person* – and the snob in you is struggling to get on board with the plastic loungers and piano bars. You don't want to spend your mornings doing aqua aerobics with the animation team, and your evenings watching magic shows. That probably makes you a horrible, pretentious person, but so be it.

For the hell of it, you try Googling some of the more upmarket holiday companies. You know you can't afford them, but maybe there's a trip to Aruba in August they can't get rid of and have decided to give away at a knock-down price. These places look swankier, granted, with a better quality of stock photo. But there's something a bit sterile about the manicured lawns and pool complexes. They look like the kind of prison you imagine Martha Stewart went to. In any case, it turns out that their idea of a special offer is not the same as yours.

So what do you do? You ask around, fishing for an invite somewhere, but your friends aren't rich enough to have holiday homes of their own, or seem to be going on villa holidays you aren't invited on. It looks like it's just you lot. Still, that will be nice, you think. Proper quality time to do the rounders/board game-type stuff you should probably have done with them throughout the year, but haven't.

But you still aren't sure where to go. The problem is that you and your children have wildly different tastes. Everything that would make them happy is too noisy and garish for your delicate sensibilities. It's like holidaying with Liberace. They, meanwhile, aren't old enough or placid enough to fit in with your family-holiday fantasies of kayaking and horse riding against idyllic backdrops.

And with children there are so many other factors you have to consider, like the weather. Naturally you don't want to go anywhere too cold, but it can't be too hot, either. If it is, then your day at the beach becomes twenty minutes at the beach before you start fretting about sunstroke and cancer. And what if it rains? What will you do then? After all, there's only so long you can spend playing Connect 4.

You realize that you've been Googling holidays for some three days now, and could spend another three weeks doing as much without getting any further. Was it always so difficult to book a holiday? You miss travel agents. Do they even still have travel agents? Because you still don't know where you're going, only that it will be a compromise: somewhere none of you really want to go.

Never leaving Europe again

Once upon a time you could have travelled anywhere. Not that you made the most of it. Russia, New Zealand, that place Mick Jagger and the Middletons like – the world is full of countries you never went to while you had the chance. And now it's too late. Because these days the world has shrunk – or for you it has, anyway.

If you have small children, the idea of a long-haul holiday can feel as achievable as a trip to Venus. Because, even barring the expense and hassle, it simply feels like too much of a risk. The more far-flung the trip, the greater the potential for disappointment. Spunk £6k on a fortnight in Rio and you're going to be gutted when it's ruined by whining, ungrateful kids. Book a leaky caravan in Northumberland and at least your expectations will be low enough for it not to matter.

But even though you know how tough it would be, part of you would love to do a big holiday with the family. It would be an adventure, something your children would remember for a lifetime (although you'd want guarantees on that – another reason to wait until they're older).

And you can tell yourself it's great for the kids. Certainly it's easier to sell yourself a big trip as being educational. Go to Mexico and you can dress it up as an opportunity to learn about indigenous peoples, ancient cultures, etc. No one's going to buy that about two weeks in Albufeira.

But the bigger the trip, the bigger the pressure. After all, you can barely go for lunch without it turning into a fiasco – what's going to happen on a long-haul trip, where day-long plane journeys and jet lag are involved?

Ah, jet lag. Anyone who's flown to a different time zone with children will remember what it's like: being exhausted to the point of collapse before finally – finally! – going to sleep, only for that to be the moment your child decides to get up for the day. It's memories like this that stay with you, like scar tissue, when the hotel pool and trip to the butterfly farm are long forgotten.

Europe it is, then. Preferably somewhere right by an airport, with no more than a two-hour flight time. But even given those criteria, it's hard to decide where to go. Everywhere recommended on Mumsnet is booked out years in advance. Everywhere recommended in magazines costs a thousand billion pounds. And you're not sure you trust your friends' recommendations, since most people's strategy for dealing with crap holidays is to just tell everyone it was amazing anyway.

So you are left trawling the internet, which takes hours and always leaves you feeling like you could've got a better deal if you'd persevered a bit longer. But you can't face typing in your dates and needs one more time only to find that the headline price was a lie, or available for two fully booked nights in January.

At least having kids forces you to expand your horizons a bit. The places you might once have turned your nose up at, such as the Canary Islands – with their reliable weather and family focus – suddenly start to sound very appealing. *What's that?* you say. *A water park? And an all-inclusive deal? Don't mind if I do, thank you very much.* Your standards are lower these days, which helps. Whereas once you might have dwelt on the quality of the nightlife or beauty of the beaches, what you're wondering now is:

a. Can you drive there?
b. Do the cheapo airlines fly there?

You find yourself drawn to places with a reputation for being nice to children – namely, Italy, Spain and Greece. Italy would be a slam-dunk, if only for the menu. They could stuff their faces with pizza, pasta and ice cream, and you could feel, for once, like you've got children who'll eat anything. But you are locked into school holidays, and Italy in school holidays costs more than your house is worth. Meanwhile, you're not quite sure where's good in Spain, and Greece always sounds like it involves too many ferries.

Wherever you go, it needs to be easy. Because for most mothers holidays are like everyday life, but with no child-care, and added sunburn and mosquitoes. Anything that makes it harder – epic journeys, visas, the non-availability of Calpol – can go to hell.

And that's how you start talking yourself around to Cornwall or Pembrokeshire. Stick to the UK and you can make your own schedule – you have the freedom to just get in the car and go. In any case, there is a moral superiority in holidaying close to home. It signals you aren't frivolous and don't waste money on fripperies. You also get the added Brucie bonus of pretending you're concerned about your carbon footprint (which secretly you sulk isn't nearly big enough). You may take this high-handedness so far that you start referring to other people's long-haul trips as 'exotic holidays'. This is a good way of masking the fact that you are dying of jealousy and no more want to go camping in Wales than you want to go to Chernobyl. There's a part of you that would genuinely rather stay at home.

But give it fifteen years or so and you'll be able to

travel again. Now you get why empty-nesters start going on cruises to Antarctica and climbing Machu Picchu. This will be you one day, making up for lost time. And it's nice to have something to look forward to, other than, y'know, senility and death. This is what you have to tell yourself, anyway. For now, you are knee-deep in Trunkis and swimming nappies. But, one day, Saga Holidays will be yours.

House swaps, Airbnb and other ways to do holidays on the cheap

The cheap getaway no longer exists once you have children. That £150 discount flight is never quite such a bargain when you have to buy it four times over. It's one of life's cruel jokes that, at the stage in life when you most deserve a holiday, you're the least able to pay for one. But it turns out that going away isn't impossible – it merely requires a little ingenuity, and the willingness to do something you'd ordinarily cross continents to avoid, like a house swap.

The first option is the house swap with friends. This can work well, if you can get past the awkwardness of suggesting it, with its implicit message that you're not so much interested in seeing your mates as staying in their gaff. The advantages here are that you know them, and that they're unlikely to use your living room for a meth-fuelled orgy. You most likely know their house – or at least that it exists – which should save you any unpleasant surprises. They won't lie to you about the distance to the

Tube or tell you that you won't hear a peep from the night-club on the corner. They will respect your belongings like they're their own.

But, as careful as they are, they may still break or damage things. Only you can't then be as annoyed about it as you could be with a stranger, who you could charge for the item or at least torment by telling them it was an irreplaceable heirloom. Friends will be more interested than any stranger would be in your mortgage statements and vibrator collection. They will be generally more curious about how you live and the state in which you keep your cutlery drawer. All of which means you'll have to spend far more time cleaning and hiding stuff than you would were you just swapping with some random off a website.

Swapping with strangers, meanwhile, may come with risks, but allows you to be more mercenary when choosing who to trade homes with. Yes, you may have a bougainvillea-clad villa in the Florida Keys, but I'll take that villa and raise you a two-bed flat in Wood Green. Because when it comes to cold, hard value, we're about evens, right? Going with strangers also broadens your options. You probably have friends in just a few select places you've already been to; you have strangers all over the world.

But there's something creepy about having a complete unknown sleep in your bed, even though when you stay in hotels it never occurs to you to question how many others have shared those same sheets. This is where Airbnb comes into its own: although you're paying for the privilege, at least you get to be the creepy stranger, rather than hosting them.

And what a boon Airbnb has turned out to be for the travelling family. Go to a hotel en masse and you're looking at a double room or a suite or some other byword for monstrously expensive. You're likely to be stuck in a small space and locked into the £16-a-head breakfast buffet. You all have to be in best-behaviour mode, as there are other guests around who don't take kindly to having a five-year-old join their table and ask to try their pudding. The pressure to be good will prove too much for some, leading to the inevitable public meltdown.

But stay in someone's flat and you can be your shouty, badly behaved selves. You can buy your own cheapskate breakfasts and not worry that the staff are judging you. Better than that, you can find somewhere bigger and swankier than the equivalent hotel, which means that you don't spend the whole stay tripping over suitcases or realize that you're all in the same room and one of you goes to bed at 7 p.m.

On the downside, Airbnbs don't tend to come with amenities – there are no pools, bars or fitness centres. When you finish dinner, you can't phone that nice man from downstairs and get him to take away your plates. In fact, there's as much cleaning and washing up as there would be at home. And because you're in someone else's house, you feel you can't leave it festering on the side. So you end up doing more than you would at home.

And, blinded by the prospect of affordable accommodation, you may have overlooked something crucial – namely that your children are vandals, liable to smash anything that isn't nailed down and plaster stickers to anything that is. When you made the booking, you only thought about your kids in terms of how much space they take up (not much), rather than how much damage they cause (loads).

All of which can be embarrassing when you get your feedback and your Airbnb host – the one who was so friendly when you were booking, and so amenable about providing a travel cot – suddenly turns nasty. 'They left greasy baby handprints on my leather dining chairs,' she writes on your review, immediately killing your chances of ever staying in another Airbnb again.

You are responsible enough to be mortified, but what's really galling is that you didn't even notice. You thought you'd left the place in pretty good shape. After all, you're a proper grown up now, who keeps important documents in a filing cabinet and has never taken nitrous oxide. You're pretty bloody boring, as it goes. And what's the point in being boring if you can't be trustworthy with it?

But it dawns on you that having kids has changed your attitude to home decor and cleanliness. While your house was never going to trouble the pages of *World of Interiors*, there were certain standards you adhered to, pre-children. Back then, you never found pear cores behind the computer or snot on the sofa. Nobody headbutted the wall and left a big chunk of plaster missing. You could have bought a cream-upholstered chair without it being the dumbest thing you ever did in your life.

Fast-forward five years and you're so used to the dirt and imperfections that you don't even notice them any more. The scribble marks on the skirting board blend in; the scratches on your desk are now, literally, part of the furniture. So when you tidy your Airbnb and think that it looks just fine, you're forgetting that other – child-free – people might not be of the same mind. Which means that you're back at hotels. Where at least they don't review you.

Boys *v* Girls

Learning more than you ever wanted to know about JCBs or How boring books for boys can be

The tableau you imagined was a cosy one: you and your son curled up in an armchair, reading tales from your own childhood: Dr Seuss, *Winnie-the-Pooh*, *Toad of Toad Hall*. Or perhaps the classics you could never actually fancy at the time, like *Gulliver's Travels* or *Treasure Island*.

But just as you hated the books your parents tried to foist on you, so he dislikes your choices, even the expensive hardbacks with the stylee retro designs that look so cool in the shop. It turns out that no child ever chooses *Animalium* or *I Want My Hat Back*. These are what adults buy to impress other adults.

What your son wants is books about transport. You never in your life imagined having to read so many. Your friend buys him a beautiful but deeply boring book about trains. It has sections called 'Types of Platform' and 'Famous Platforms of the World'. This is too old for him, you think. His thirst for locomotive data cannot run that deep. You are wrong.

And so you find yourself reading it night after night.

You learn about diesel engines and exactly how points work. You discover that Kharagpur Station in India has the longest platform in the world (over 1K). You come to know as much about planes, rockets, buses, trucks, tractors and just about every other kind of vehicle. Soon you are able to tell a haul truck from a flatbed at forty paces.

In a bid to change the subject, you buy him the Mr Men books, because a discount site is doing the complete set for thirty quid. It works! He likes them! But there are fifty of them, and they are all basically the same. It becomes clear there is a formula: Mr Man has a defining characteristic (greedy, lazy, grumpy, etc.). He meets someone with the opposing trait and goes to stay with him, where he learns to modify his behaviour. Roger Hargreaves got fifty books out of that, you think. Children's books are a wheeze. You decide you're going to write one, just as soon as you have an idea. You wonder how much you will make from the merchandise.

Other books are plain weird. *Thomas the Tank Engine*, an early obsession with many boys, comes in two main forms: dull board books where the writer doesn't even pretend to bother with a story, and the original Reverend W. Awdry books, which are lesser known. You soon learn why. In one tale, Henry is reluctant to ruin his new paint job in the rain. As punishment for his vanity, he is bricked up in a tunnel for ever. The story ends with the words: 'He is very sad because no one will ever see his lovely green paint with red stripes again. But I think he deserved it, don't you?' You vow not to read any more children's books written by clergy.

You go to the library, congratulating yourself on your

thrift and civic-mindedness the whole way there. Here you are, supporting your local library, making sure it doesn't close. Take that, austerity cuts. Two months later you discover that you took the kids' books out on an adult card and could have bought them three times over with what you owe in fines. You never go to the library again.

But you persist in buying books because it's an easy way to feel like a good parent, even if it ends in an argument about why the *Power Rangers Annual* doesn't count. You show your age by being slightly suspicious of the Gruffalos of this world, feeling more comfortable with the Janet and Allan Ahlbergs and Jan Pieńkowskis of your own childhood. When your kids get into *Cops and Robbers* or *Funnybones* or *Meg and Mog*, it feels like a small personal triumph. Not only are you instilling a love of reading, you're instilling a love of *old books*. Hooray for you.

Then they get older and the transport books are relegated in favour of those about aliens and space, and suddenly you know more about the solar system than you ever did. You find yourself hoping you can use this information in some way – that someone might happen to wonder how many moons Jupiter has, so you can tell them: 'Why, it has over sixty.' But no one ever asks you that.

Still, you suppose you should enjoy it while it lasts, because there will come a day when he is locking you out of his room so he can read about things you *do* have some knowledge of. Or watch them online, anyway.

Girls' World and other toys you probably shouldn't buy but do

Today's mothers grew up in a world of everyday sexism, where women in sequined G-strings held up playing cards and danced with an old man and they called it family entertainment. The feminine ideal we were led to aspire to sat somewhere between Lady Di, Kylie Minogue and Delia Smith.

And our toys propagated this vision. They were the merchandise for the kind of women we were expected to grow into. Hairdressing heads and play kitchens. Busty blondes in sports cars. Fantasy ponies and caring bears. Babies that weed. These were the things we coveted, and we loved them with all our hearts, didn't we, girls? Who doesn't recall the mesmerizing joy of her Sindy house, which came with its own cutlery and a shower that pumped real water? Who didn't Biro over their Girls' World's face and braid their My Little Pony's tail over and over? Who didn't love her Strawberry Shortcake doll like it was her own flesh and blood?

So it's a tough call when you find yourself the mother of a daughter, here in the twenty-first century. Your eyes have been opened since your own childhood. The penny has dropped. You've realized that, no, it's not fair that you don't get paid the same as the boys. And no, you don't really fancy making breakfast, lunch and dinner for everyone, every day for evermore, thanks all the same. Women have been busy redefining themselves, in your very lifetime. And what with feminism being all trendy and that, it seems like this time round even the men are starting to agree.

But as a mother today, you are caught between two worlds: your own childhood and the one you want your daughter to have. Yes, you are all about raising a strong, independent woman, who doesn't feel she needs to conform to stereotypes or be judged on her looks to succeed. You want her to have a sense of self-worth and inner poise, feel like she can do whatever she wants to do, and certainly whatever her brother does. You want dignity and respect for her, equal pay and opportunities. Admittedly, you haven't quite mastered some of these things yourself yet, but you can see they could come in handy for a girl these days.

But, man, you want to give her a Girls' World, too. Because you used to play with yours for hours. In fact, you want to share and pass on to her all the things you loved as a little girl. You want to teach her how to do French plaits and cat's cradles. You want to take her roller-skating and show her *Bagpuss*. You want her to have a big box of ribbons and hairbands, all mixed up, like the one you used to have. You want her to feel the same wonder you felt the first time you saw Cinderella's blue dress in the Ladybird *Well-Loved Tales* book. Bake the butterfly cakes from the *My Learn to Cook Book*. Have the peach Care Bear. Generally be the exact same little girl that you were. Freud's probably got a name for it.

But that's no good, is it, woman? Giving your daughter a head of blonde synthetic hair and some brushes to play with doesn't send the right message to today's young lady at all. Would you even remotely consider giving your son the same thing? Can you imagine the look on his face as he unwrapped his Boys' World head, complete with play-clippers and diamond earring? Actually, that's quite a good idea . . .

But maybe it is OK to give her a Girls' World? After all, being a modern feminist doesn't mean dropping femininity altogether, right? Perhaps it's fine, as long as you counter it with something less gender-stereotypey, like a box of K'nex, for example. Give her a broad experience. But you know already that no seven-year-old daughter of yours is going to put down the hair-colouring pens to make a K-Force Build and Blast gun. And yes, you know there are those special girls' ranges, like Lego Friends. But they don't sit well with you either. Why should a construction toy have to be pink and involve puppies to get a girl to play with it? And God, it's exhausting being righteous.

So you go round and round in big sparkly circles, never quite sure of what message you're trying to send her via the medium of toys. And it pisses you off a bit that her toys have to carry a message at all. They don't seem to be just toys, like your son's. You will probably never stress about the Hot Wheels truck your son got for Christmas being too boyish. Whereas the nail-art kits and princess dresses she gets – they are loaded guns, full of fluffy, sexualized bullets.

So you go for a mixed-message approach. She gets a Barbie Bubbletastic Mermaid Doll one Christmas, and a bow and arrows the next. She has a My Little Pony (Rainbow Dash, who at least has primary-coloured accessories), but instead of the Elsa dress she really wants, she gets a doctor's outfit. You're not sure this is the right approach – in fact, you sometimes worry you are confusing the hell out of the poor child – but you do at least invest thought into curating her toys, fine-tuning the childhood experience that you know she will internalize and take with her through life. You do all of this, until one day you notice that she never really plays much with *any* of her toys. And you realize that's because her generation has something yours never had – the iPad.

Finding – and losing – your inner soccer mom

When you were growing up, watching your dad watching the football on television gave you the idea that here was the most boring thing to do in the world. The droning crowd, with its uncivilized chants and relentless clackers, came to represent the sound of hell to you. Given the choice, you'd rather sit through *Songs of Praise* than see those ugly men with bad skin chase a ball around a field. Seriously, what was the point? Why did everyone get so excited about A GAME?

So it was a surprise to discover how much you enjoyed watching your son play football. Once he was old enough to join, Saturday mornings were all about Little Kickers. This was a pain because it started at 9 a.m., and was especially difficult if you'd overdone it on the wine the night before. But you were prepared to accept the inconvenience if it helped him. Sport is so important, you'd tell your mum, as if she'd never heard of it before. Not just for their health, but social skills. The teamwork, winning and losing, taking part. So important, all that stuff.

He started supporting Manchester United and took an interest in the charts or leagues or whatever they're called. He began collecting Match Attax cards and books with titles like *1,000 World Soccer Records*, where he learned interesting facts about Lionel Messi's average match score and how much Gareth Bale's last car cost. That's good, you'd tell your mother again, who couldn't care less and only wanted to talk about her friend Joan's sciatica. Because it's mathematical, all those numbers and tables. It appeals to his mathematical brain.

You'd heard about soccer moms in America – these women who tirelessly drive their kids to sporting activities. And you were going to be one of them – his biggest fan. Nothing would stop you supporting his love of the game. Here was confirmation that you were a good parent. You had a fine, sporting son, who could score goals in football. And as a bonus, you fancied the coach, who had lovely legs. Never seen such nice legs on a man.

Allowing yourself to feel smug, you put aside your ambivalent feelings about the corrupt, sexist, multi-billion-pound football industry and how image-led and materialistic it is. And how it is just a game, albeit of two halves. You put that aside because your son was showing talent and you saw pound signs. Three hundred grand a week, Wayne Rooney earns, and he doesn't even look like he's in good shape. And that lovely Lionel Messi got a tattoo of his mum on his back and bought her a mansion.

So you're all for it when he joins the local youth team, which means training on Friday evenings through winter and a ninety-minute wait in the car for you as it isn't worth going home. Then the big local team – the one you've actually heard of – scouts your son for their youth academy. Recognition at last! This means more training on Monday nights, forty-five minutes away, in the excuse for a city the club calls home. Season fees are £65, and, oh, can you buy the kit? It's £45. And can he take part in a football festival next Saturday? He'll be needed for six hours.

His dad wants to take him, but you insist on doing it as you want him to know that mums can be into football too. And you enjoy it – every silky pass he makes is proof of your superlative parenting, after all. You notice that not many other mums come – it's mostly dads – but this is further evidence of your commitment to your son's now-inevitable career in football. You are a sporting tiger mother, like that Andy Murray's mum.

He needs new boots, for the special AstroTurf they play on these days. This is on top of the regular stud boots, school trainers and gym pumps. Plus the normal everyday trainers for the moments of his life that he isn't playing football. So that's five pairs of trainers, for one child? He wants Nike Hypervenoms, the price of which makes you feel like a granny, muttering about how much Clarks has improved recently. And please can he have a Barcelona kit with his name on the back? They only cost £75.

Oh, and being in the club means playing matches on Sundays, too. Often in a municipal field in a small, depressing town on the other side of the county. There's no team bus, so can you have him there for 8.30 a.m. ON SUNDAY to warm up? Dutifully, you watch these matches in the drizzle. There are no seats, or retro half-time oranges. It's you and some grimacing dads in fleeces, who take it very seriously and shout at their sons about getting into space and releasing earlier. Secretly, you are questioning the wisdom of getting your son into football.

Because it's starting to feel like all take and no give, this soccer-mom schtick. What with the thrice-weekly training and whole weekends spent driving to fields. And it's costing a fortune, when you take into account the footwear collection, the personalized kit, socks, shin pads, branded kit bags and drinks bottles. Bloody Match Attax cards all over the bloody house, and the magazines filled with articles about whose wife has the most expensive engagement ring. You are falling out of love with football.

Add to that the crooked industry, predatory players and negative messages these WAGs send young girls, perhaps he'd have been better off joining a choir or trying archery instead? But it's too late, you've lost him. He's bought into the dream and you gave him the ticket.

You tot up the hours that lie before you, of standing on muddy goal lines and reading Facebook in car parks on Monday nights in February, and wonder if your support might be called for elsewhere. Watching your daughter dance, for example, in the centrally heated theatre – the one with seats and a cafe. And isn't this a brilliant opportunity for father and son to spend quality time together? Perhaps you should take this one for the team and surrender your services. You text his dad: *Can you take him to football tonight?*

Giving in to pink

Before you had her, when you had this motherhood lark sussed, you plonked yourself right up there on the moral high ground in a massive righteous huff about pink. You would not be dressing your little girl in pink. Or decorating her room in pink or having pink toys or doing anything stupid and girly and pink. Your daughter's childhood would not be stereotyped and generally made a patsy of by the evil-minded patriarchs who pedal this stuff as part of their master-plan to keep women in the kitchen.

The way things have gone is outrageous, you inform your baffled parents, who make the mistake of suggesting you might enjoy dressing your new baby girl in pink dresses. Back in your ballerina music box, old, unreconstructed relatives! This is tough, modern mother you are talking to here. You played with gender-specific toys as a child, it's true. You had a toy Hoover, yes. But it sure as hell wasn't pink and called Henrietta. Why can't girls be free to be girls? Why does everything have to be pink? You follow Pink Stinks on Twitter and roll your eyes at all the pink things in the shops. Your mum is terrified of you.

And, credit where it's due, you give standing up to pink your best shot. When she's born and the fuchsia outfits and flower-shaped hats pour in from well-meaning well-wishers, you take them back and exchange them for neutral alternatives.

Playgroups become a sort of anti-pink demonstration. Each week at Kindermusik, which she usually sleeps through, you notice that everyone is dressing their daughters in increasingly esoteric colour combinations. There's a lot of purple. Sometimes there is so much purple, you wonder if it isn't the new pink. But you hold your own with mid-century shades of mustard and teal. She wears dungarees and her brother's old wellies with motorcycles on. She has an Iggle Piggle toy. Seriously, what more can you do?

But despite your efforts, you know you are doomed. It's too confusing. If she can't wear pink because it sends the wrong message about gender stereotypes, you should probably stop wearing make-up and skirts. That's the logical conclusion of this logic, isn't it? Is that right? Or is it still OK to wear lipstick? Can someone please check *How To Be a Woman*?

Whatever Caitlin says, the no-lipstick thing isn't going to happen. You feel old and ugly enough as it is. The irony of which is not lost on you, but kind of put to one side while you do a face mask.

She's cottoned on now, anyway. All she wants to do is dress up as a princess and make perfume from rose petals. You have a moan about this to your mother, who thinks this is perfectly normal behaviour for a little girl. You loved doing that when you were that age. And you launch into an ill-thought-out rant about how you could argue that wearing perfume sends the message to young girls that women smell. The Chanel No. 5 bottle isn't a design classic, it's the iconography of patriarchal abuse. Your mother is now so confused by you, she vows to give you only vouchers for Christmas from this day on. You can choose what you want then. She doesn't know what you like any more.

As you are raging against the machine, your daughter is kidnapped by Disney aliens and replaced with Elsa from *Frozen*. She will only wear dresses, even to bed, and tells everyone she meets that growing her hair is her favourite thing to do. She's now choosing her own outfits, too, which always involve unacceptable amounts of sequins and head-to-toe pink. Thanks to all the brilliant birthday presents she gets, her nails are permanently painted in pink glitter gel and she has a pair of dressing-up high heels with pink fluffy bits on – just like a real sex kitten. Sometimes you catch her, mesmerized by her own image in the mirror. She's doing something bizarre. Is that . . . raunchy dancing?

Clearly, your standards are slipping. This is in no small way due to the fact that you are too busy deciding what to wear, cleaning the house and cooking the tea to fight about it. Another irony that is not lost on you. But you put it aside with the lipstick, while you unwrap the new silk blouse with the plunging neckline that you won on eBay. It's pink.

And when the time comes to decorate her bedroom, she begs you to paint it pink. And perhaps because a dark part of you secretly quite likes the idea, or because you don't want her to feel left out as all her friends' rooms are pink, or because you're too tired to fight about it and no longer give a shit about this stupid colour, you let her have her bloody pink bedroom. And it dawns on you that this is why Farrow & Ball have a whole page of classy pinks with names like Calamine and Nancy's Blushes, so that nice, liberal-minded mothers like you can give in to pink and pass it off as good taste.

Losing Your Cool

Secretly liking out-of-town shopping villages

You know the shops you're supposed to like: the quirky independents fighting the good fight against the faceless chains, the ones saving our high streets from becoming clones lined with 4,000 branches of Pret.

And it's true – you do love these places and everything they stand for. To the point that you feel really bad every time you go into one, see something you like and then buy it later on Amazon. You know how tough life is for small shops, which makes you feel guilty for wasting their time by hanging around, looking at tea-light holders you've got no intention of buying.

The trouble with small shops is that they can make you feel a bit awkward. Sometimes you just want to browse, but it's embarrassing to walk out empty-handed. It can feel like a snub to the person behind the counter, especially when they've been so friendly and made a point of showing you all the new stock. Granted, this doesn't usually take long – it's amazing how well these places seem to do, given that so many stock little more than four hand-carved wooden spoons and a £7 ball of string. It can mean you find yourself craving choice, and anonymity. That said, the answer isn't usually a giant mall, what with all those teenagers and people stopping you to ask if they can ask you a question about your hair.

Luckily for you, there's a third way: the out-of-town shopping village. You know the accepted line on these: they are soulless, characterless places straight out of Stepford. You concede that, with their clock towers and weather vanes, they can sometimes err on the twee side. And maybe the fountains and easy-listening tunes pumped from hidden speakers are a step too Disney.

But, while you know there's something quintessentially naff and Shires-y about them, the faux-village veneer has its appeal. A part of you likes the idea of the small-town American idyll they're trying to recreate, the one you grew up seeing in films. After all, this is the closest most of us Brits will ever get to going to the Hamptons or Nantucket. No, we might not have the pumpkin patches or chowder shacks, but we do have a branch of Thomas Pink in a clapboard barn.

And there's usually a lot of effort that's gone into these places – someone's thought to landscape the gardens and fence off the A-road. They have nice toilets and you never have to walk too far to the cafe. Often there's some kind of playground or carousel-type affair to keep the kids happy. Although in truth they had you at convenient parking.

Out-of-town shopping villages tend to stock quality, unthreatening brands you know where you are with. There's nothing too edgy or directional – you won't find yourself intimidated by the music or baffled by the jewellery. While this isn't the place for bleeding-edge fashion, you'll probably get a deal on Le Creuset and some fluffy towels. They're ideal for stocking up your present drawer (because you aspire to be the kind of woman who has a present drawer).

They're especially good in the run-up to Christmas, when they've usually gone to town on the whole festive thing, with giant fir trees wrapped in fairy lights and velvet ribbon. You'll often find the whole place decked out with the kind of campy, vintage-style baubles you want to decorate your own house with, until you find out that they're £10 apiece and you'll need thirty of them for it to look any good.

But there's something comfortable and safe about out-of-town shopping villages all year round. They're clean and well maintained. There are no Cashinos or William Hills or other gloomy reminders that you live in the real world. They're often packed with coachloads of Chinese tourists on the hunt for a bargain, which is reassuring. Yes, you've travelled fifteen miles, but they've come all the way from Guangdong, so it must be good.

Compared to your average high street, with its pollution and petty crime, places like this feel positively wholesome. Honestly, anyone would think they were designed with mothers in mind. You can bring your children and tell yourself it's like going for a country walk, only with a more diverting backdrop. So you get to look round the shops, while the kids have an outing – it's two birds, one stone. You are one great mother. With some new cast-iron bakeware to boot.

Dancing like a mum

As a young, single lady with a job, and a salary to spend on fripperies like earrings and M&S meals-for-one, music and nightclubs were the centre of your world. Whole weekends were constructed around whichever DJ was playing his records at whichever superclub. Here, you would willingly queue for three hours to get to the door, where your attractiveness and level of cool would be assessed by a shouty clipboard Nazi, and you would be granted entrance, all for twenty quid – the sort of sum that at the time would have covered your weekly shop (back when your basics were Supernoodles, fags and a four-pack of Milky Bar yoghurts).

Some of your Best. Nights. Ever. have been spent in those clubs, on those podiums, in those chill-out rooms. Gurning your face off like a camel and chain-smoking, while trying to focus and telling the stranger next to you they had lovely teeth. Looking back, it's no surprise you never had a boyfriend.

But, frankly, there wasn't room for one in your crazy, happy life. You were too busy dancing somewhere – on some terrace, in some tunnel, hands in the air like you just didn't care. And you thought you were quite a good dancer, as it goes. You had a few signature moves, some shapes you liked to throw down. On top of your naturally rhythmic sway, you had a spot of batty-shaking, some arm-waving and clapping, a little bit of running man if you were feeling brave. Always plenty of whooping and trilling when the beat kicked in. You could lean forward, shimmy your shoulders and click your fingers, lean back and throw your forearms in and out like you were feeding the pigeons in Trafalgar Square. Girl, you could ride de riddim.

Then the babies started coming in and you were grounded. The dancing stopped and it was time to get down off the podium, exit the club.

Your days were spent moving slowly from bed to sofa to cafe to soft mat at the leisure centre. When you eventually started socializing again, it was all sit-down dinners and girls' nights out in poncey cocktail bars with chocolate-brown leather sofas. Apart from the occasional drunken kitchen disco with the kids, dancing just wasn't part of your life any more.

So it's a funny thing when the fortieths (and fiftieths) and the odd late wedding begin to kick in. These are the big parties that have a massive build-up, that you discuss every detail of with your friends. The ones where you might ship the kids to Grandma's for the weekend, or get an overnight babysitter, because you're going to really let your now-full-head-of-highlights hair down. The ones where you think hard about what you're going to wear, because even though you're married, there might be a new fit dad there you can flirt with. Nothing wrong with a bit of window shopping – eh, ladies?

The night comes and they've hired some barn or a big house, and it's all new tops from Reiss and fairy lights in the marquee and Prosecco on arrival. Your mate's friend from London is DJ-ing, and he used to play at a club that you pretend you went to loads, so that's cool. And you all stand around the organic hog roast and tell each other how great you look, while making snide comments about mutton to your other half, who appears to have fallen in love with the hog roast and rarely leaves its side all night. All the while, you are inserting free Prosecco, trying to achieve the level of wild abandon required to hit the dance floor.

Your moment arrives. It's 'Blue Monday', or maybe 'California Soul' – one of those club classics that's cool enough to be acceptable to a savvy ageing raver like you, but mainstream enough to fill the floor with regular ageing people, too – and you do the half-dance-half-walk thing to the dance floor and start to get moving. You're going to show these people just how old school you are. You're going to let them know, via the medium of dance, exactly where you're coming from. Back in the day. Oh, yeah, baby.

But something feels wrong. Your basic natural sway is still there, but when you think about bringing out the running man, you feel kind of awkward. Something inside tells you that to do the sexy leaning-forward-clicking-fingers-shimmy would make you look a bit like your aunty and uncle did when they sat down to 'Oops Upside Your Head'. You raise your arms a little bit, but realize that to pump them up and down like you did when Andy Weatherall dropped a fat one that time in 'Beefa would be kind of inappropriate here in your mate's parents' garden. You shake your batty a little, but you know that's not necessarily a good look for you these days, even in these new £150 arse-sculpting jeans.

So you end up performing a routine based largely on your aerobics class: side-stepping and doing what is essentially the grapevine, while biting your lip to show you are really into this groove, man. Your arms stay at waist height and you click your fingers in a way that makes you look not unlike one of the Supremes. You are disappointed to note that you feel like a club-footed old frump. Worse, no one is admiring your moves. Occasionally you do a comedy, ironic version of the dancing you used to do, just to let others know where your hip social references lie. Your old moves may be staying in their box, but after all that Prosecco, your thirst for attention knows no slaking.

By this time, however, you are being completely upstaged by the dads, who are getting busy over there, reliving their own glory days. A bunch of fat, sweaty, balding men are doing painful-looking windmills and swan dives, collectively imagining they are the Sugar Hill Gang. One of them has taken over the mic and is trying to do the rap, but is making a sound more like the noise you get when you accidentally dial a fax machine. Another is being carried off by the host's dad, his nose bleeding after forgetting to put his hands down before a caterpillar.

Now fully lubricated and keen to get kudos of any kind at this stage, you decide that to divert attention back to yourself, you will need to do something drastic. So you pull out the only trick left up your sleeve – the splits – a move you have never been able to do, but like to think you can every time you get on the Prosecco. And, for one glorious moment, the floor is yours. Everyone is so out of their mind they don't notice your crotch is nowhere near the ground, and whoop and cheer at your incredible feat. Either that, or they are shrieking in awkward astonishment at what you seem to be doing down there. Whichever it is, you feel pleased to be acknowledged for something, even if it is a shit attempt at a gymnastics manoeuvre.

Struggling to get up, Prosecco all over the now less-sculpted arse of your new jeans, you glimpse your partner. He's standing at the side of the dance floor, pork roll in hand, giving you the 'not this again' look. And you know it's time to go home. Still got it though, girl. Oh, yes.

Going a bit Etsy

Before a certain age, extra-curricular activities are some-thing you make up for your CV, because the truth – that you spend your time eating, sleeping and drinking – is unlikely to knock out a potential employer. But there comes a time in life when you find yourself drawn to the type of old-people hobbies more kindly referred to as 'crafting'. In other words, it all starts to go a bit Etsy.

One reason for this is that now, more than ever, you need an outlet. In the old days, that might have been partying. But now, though you've possibly got it in you to stay up all night, you can't do that *and* the other stuff that's expected of you, like parenting.

It's around this time that many women find themselves hit with the urge for self-improvement. Some go crazy for exercise and start running marathons (see also: Marathons, triathlons and other midlife crises, p. 166). Others find sanity in blogging, upcycling furniture, choir groups or cross-stitching profanities. It doesn't really matter what it is, just that it offers an escape, and a sense that you might find your niche. Who knows? Maybe you were always meant to be a taxidermist or a quilt maker.

Plus, this is the new, busy you, who has to be doing something all the time, even if it's emptying the dishwasher or neatening the rising piles of crap on the sideboard. Who takes a certain martyrish pride in never sitting down. Finding a hobby serves your need to be productive, even when you're slacking off.

And you're at a stage in life when the term 'me time' gets bandied about a lot. The question is – when you finally get some, what are you going to do with it? The phrase suggests massages and manicures, but you can only have so many of those without bankrupting yourself, so it's worth finding something you enjoy that doesn't involve paying a salon a great wad of cash.

And activities like knitting and gardening enable you to produce something tangible. They're also good creative outlets for people who aren't very gifted creatively. Take up painting watercolours and there's a strong chance you're going to embarrass yourself. Doing GCSE art told you all you need to know about your talent for it. But who knows? You might just be a genius at the old crochet or embroidery. And so few people these days are handy with a needle, you're likely to be applauded for your talents and your championing of forgotten skills.

But there's a practical element, too. Who knew that children's trousers got so holey? Didn't you only buy them a fortnight ago? *I must sew a patch on those*, you think, before remembering you can't sew and writing their names on their uniforms in Sharpie pen rather than stitch in name labels – an act your own mother would have considered an unthinkable cheat.

It isn't just patches though. If you knew how to sew, you could make your daughter those floral bloomers and smock dresses that posh shops charge £££ for – the ones you see and huff, 'I could do that,' knowing you couldn't. You could make your own curtains and cushions, instead of being skanked by department stores. You get carried away and start imagining yourself knocking up children's clothes made from original 1970s patterns, which you can then sell online.

The downside to sewing is that there are certain barriers to entry – i.e. you need a sewing machine. And you just know this is only going to end up gathering dust with the juicer, the exercise ball and the slow cooker. Besides, if you had £100 burning a hole in your pocket, you could think of a hundred more fun things to buy than a sewing machine.

Knitting – if you can get the hang of it – is more easily accessed and means you can make everyone a scarf for Christmas while getting to watch a lot of TV. Because the beauty of old-people's hobbies is that they give you the chance to be idle, yet still have something to show for it. They give you something to talk about at a time of life when you have nothing to say. They help you to get out and meet people, and provide opportunities for showing off, as you flaunt your homemade artisanal bread or four-tier vanilla rose cake.

Even if you draw the line at making stuff, you may still find yourself appreciating old-people things. The twentysomethings are Instagramming pictures of themselves in the dancer pose on a beach at sunset. You, meanwhile, are posting pictures of wildflower meadows and your California lilac in full bloom.

Though there's something appealing about the idea of re-appropriating traditional hobbies. It feels ironic, because there's such a distance between you and old people, right? You find this highly amusing until you remember that, to vast swathes of the population, you *are* old.

The other beauty of old-people's hobbies, of course, is that there are just so many of them – there's bound to be one that appeals. Beekeeping, chicken-rearing, trug-making – activities like this give you the chance to feel like you're quietly saving the earth in your own pioneer-woman way. Along with a whole pile of kit to eBay when you admit that they aren't for you.

Talking like a dick

When you were young, you sometimes overheard parents in shops, and other places where they allow families to roam freely, threatening their children with something called 'time out'. And you would sneer at this naff Americanism, and vow never to let yourself sound like such a total muppet in public.

But, as with many of the things you said you'd never do as a mother (let them sleep in your bed; wear anything from Hobbs), you let your guard down. One day, as you attempt to reason with the three-year-old who is headbutting the floor in Pizza Express, you hear yourself talking.

And you realize you could slam any parent in this place with your arsenal of embarrassing words and phrases.

It begins when you read in baby books about concepts such as 'dream feed' and 'tummy time'. You try throwing out a couple of these to your health visitor, as part of your strategy to make her think you're doing it right. Although they sound a bit twattish, you reason to no one in particular, they are at least vaguely medical terms with vaguely medical connotations. Finding them well received, your confidence grows, and you wonder if having a bit of the lingo isn't a good thing after all. Like that time you got off with a German guy on holiday and, although he couldn't speak a word of English, when he said in his sexy German voice, 'Let's fuck,' it was really very effective.

Where were we? Oh, yes.

So you may have already dipped a toe in the waters of pretentious vocabulary, but it's only when you start to grapple with the challenging behaviours of your toddler that you really begin to develop and hone the vocabulary of arse-clenching words and phrases that truly make you sound like a dick.

Whether you put all your hopes in Supernanny or opt for a parenting course at your local children's centre, you soon find yourself briefing your deviant child on high-minded concepts such as 'special time', 'time out', 'quiet time' and other powerful time-centric terms.

Discovering that, to control your child, you basically need to add 'time' to the word of your choice, fills you with the conviction of someone born again. You don't care if you sound like a halfwit, this new language can bring a great peace upon your home.

You may even go so far as to draft posters detailing House Rules that are unfathomable to adults, never mind the four-year-old. These include phrases such as 'kind hands' (real meaning: *don't hit your sister*) and 'gentle voices' (*stop telling me I'm a poo-poo*). You may pretend you want him to help you decorate it, but your spirited child ends up drawing big black lines over it and sticks the smiley faces in the wrong place. So you do it all again when he goes to bed, so that it looks nice on the kitchen wall and your friends feel jealous that you have such a talented child.

So convinced are you of the power of your new-found words and phrases, it is grounds for divorce if a bewildered partner says them wrong or, worse, too loudly. It's not unusual to hear yourself shrieking: 'YOU'RE SUPPOSED TO SAY IT IN A QUIET VOICE!!!' while the child you are positively parenting takes his willy out and wees in the pair of your shoes sitting next to him on the stairs.

And God forbid anyone should call the time-out step the naughty step. For using words such as naughty is, as we all know, negative reinforcement, and there will be none of this in your new world order.

As the kids grow, you begin to take them on play dates (you just give in and say it). Later, you ask, in all seriousness, if it is wine o'clock, and discuss rearing free-range children and painting your house in Mole's Breath. And you grow so accustomed to talking like a dick, eventually you forget you are doing it at all.

Fortunately, like most of this stuff, speaking in these tongues is just another phase we go through. Once the children start school and have new ways to piss you off – lying on the floor in their pants just as it's time to leave the house, losing their new uniform on the first day of term – you can revert to traditional high-pitched shouting. You find comfort in the familiar platitudes of your own childhood, like 'how many times do I have to tell you' and 'wait till Daddy hears about this', along with threats to do terrible things that everyone knows you are too tired and busy to ever follow through with.

It's not a nice way to talk, but at least you don't sound like a dick.

Taking them to festivals

One of the great disappointments of motherhood is realizing a couple of years in that you are not the parent you planned to be. 'I will be fun mum,' you decided in the years before you had kids. 'That picture of Princess Diana with William and Harry on the log flume at Thorpe Park – that'll be me, all great teeth and hair that doesn't go frizzy when it's wet.'

So it comes as a blow when you turn out to be nagging, haranguing mum, who doesn't really like building Lego helicopters and screeches 'Just go to sleep!' when they call for you after 8 p.m. You are not laugh-a-minute, glamorous mum, but ordinary mum, who moans about laundry and knows all the words to the CBeebies Bedtime Hour song.

All those wholesome activities you thought you'd do together – the bike rides through sun-dappled forests, the crabbing in rock pools – somehow never materialize, as instead you find yourself schlepping to yet another toy library or trying to persuade them it'll be a right laugh buying eye cream in Debenhams.

But there's one time of year when you're offered the chance to be another kind of mum. For a weekend, at least, you can be Bohemian mum, whose kids run barefoot and face-painted through wildflower meadows, wearing one of those Native American headdress things that may or may not be racist.

Event organizers have cottoned on to this, which is why there are now no end of festivals aimed partly or even exclusively at kids: Camp Bestival, Elderflower Fields, Port Eliot, that one with Jamie Oliver's and Alex James's big cheesy faces splashed all over it – they're springing up all over the place. Once again, as a mother, you have become a marketeer's wet dream.

And, you've got to confess, it's tempting. For an admittedly steep ticket price, you get a whole weekend's entertainment, with no TV and a bunch of smug photos for Facebook to boot. You may have reservations about the idea of camping in festival conditions with two insomniac under-fives, but that's all part of the experience. You are hardy, you are outdoorsy, you are a creative free spirit. Go, you.

So you rock up at your festival, every inch of the car packed with sleeping bags and cool boxes and God knows what kind of crap. Then it dawns on you that getting said crap from car park to campsite with small children in tow is going to be a mission of *Challenge Anneka*-style proportions. And you realize that, despite your rammed-to-the-rafters car, you are in fact totally unprepared and disorganized, and that other people here have actually packed wheelbarrows for this purpose.

Nor did it occur to you to practise setting up the tent you borrowed, so as the seasoned campers whip up their stylish bell tents (accessorized with kilims, sheepskins and lanterns) in the blink of an eye, you are still there two hours later, wondering which pole goes into which hole and why the hell anybody does this for fun.

And you can forget about going to see anything. Bands, with their loud music and beery crowds, are a no-no with young kids. Nor will children love the line-up at posh festivals, the ones where grey-haired people you don't recognize talk about books you haven't read in Arabian tents kitted out with William Morris-print deckchairs. Comedy, too, is risky, as you find out when your wide-eyed offspring emerges from the crowd and asks loudly, 'Mummy, what's fingered?'

Feeding them costs a fortune. Everything you brought in the cool box looks grim on arrival and your suggestion of a falafel burger is greeted with theatrical vomming noises. You are reduced to begging the purveyor of hand-made artisan cheeses to make your kids the plainest, most basic Cheddar sandwich he can muster, for which he charges you £6.

Indeed, festivals will prove to be a bit like holidays, where it doesn't work until you accept that the things *you* enjoy doing simply aren't going to happen. If you're lucky, you might get a ten-minute window to read the paper while pretending to watch them take part in a drumming workshop. Because it only really succeeds once you look on the bright side. After all, that's ten minutes more than you'd normally get.

Refusing to accept that some women just don't want children

If there's one thing the media's not short of, it's articles by child-free women writing about how happy they are, and how they really don't want children, and would everybody please just naff off and leave them alone about it? You find yourself reading these pieces with a certain curiosity. They offer a *Sliding Doors* view of the life you could have had if you'd turned right instead of left.

And, sure enough, it sounds pretty fabulous – all weekend breaks and lie-ins, and the ability to nip to New York at a moment's notice. Accompanying these articles will be a photograph of the writer looking blow-dried and depilated, wearing something tight and expensive from a cult label you're not cool enough to know about. 'Why would I want to sacrifice my career and body for some squalling newborn?' she asks. 'Why would I jack in the life I love, when I've no desire to have babies?' Why indeed, you think. You'd be mad. Bet you change your mind when you hit forty-two.

Because, despite your whingeing and your weight gain – despite the fact that your whole life makes you a walking advert for contraception – you struggle to process the idea that someone would willingly forego the experience of having children. You look at your dirty, snotty offspring, the one who demands to watch movies on your iPhone at 5.30 a.m. and throws a fit in the street because you bought him the wrong kind of doughnut. Why on earth would someone want to miss out on that, you wonder?

Your mind flashes to the lazy weekends at country-house hotels, the trips to exotic places, the disposable income. Pah, holidays are all very well, but the novelty of that soon wears off, you tell yourself, sounding like some old bag in a house dress from a Les Dawson sketch. You think of the child-free women you know, with their Net-a-Porter deliveries and early-morning yoga classes, and decide that their lives are superficial, like your own is so much more meaningful because your hair looks like shit.

You don't want to be that awful person who asks every woman over thirty-two, 'So, are you thinking babies, then?' Because, as you and they and everybody else knows, women like that are a fucking nightmare and rude to boot. But it's so hard to resist, because maybe they don't want babies or can't have them. Either way, there's a story there. And while nice you knows that it's none of your business and is possibly a painful subject for them, nosy you *just wants to know*. Because why aren't they having babies? Why? WHY??

If you want to keep your friends, you have to rein in this kind of behaviour. You have to check the impulse to remind your gay friends that they can adopt, like they didn't already know that. You have to curb the instinct to drop crass hints like, 'Lola in Johnny's class has two mummies and it's SO COOL.'

Because you know that no one's looking at you and

thinking, 'She makes motherhood look such fun,' you worry that you might be putting your child-free friends off the experience altogether. So you feel compelled to compensate, banging on about how great and amazing it all is. With any luck, you stop short of saying, 'Go on, have babies. Go onnnnnnn!' but the damage is done. They know exactly what you're doing and think you're an idiot.

Your friend may patiently explain that babies aren't for her, and that she's happy enough as she is, thanks all the same. Of course, you nod, chasing your toddler between the tables in the pub garden and wondering why she insisted on coming here when it *clearly* isn't child-friendly. 'Sorry,' you pant on your return. 'What was that you were saying? No wine for me, thanks, I've got to get the kids home.' And as you part company, you wonder once again why she doesn't want babies. Ah, well, you think, she'll change her mind.

Really wanting a garage, and other suburban fantasies you can't shake

From Margot Leadbetter to Beverly in *Abigail's Party*, suburban women have come in for some stick over the years. But there's a Hyacinth Bouquet inside all of us, one who secretly likes the idea of cream shag-pile carpets and a whirlpool bath.

You might have spent your whole life trying to escape suburbia, but it turns out it wasn't so bad after all. Because even if you find yourself glamming it up in some slick city apartment, we bet you'll still find yourself hankering after at least one of the following:

1. A garage

Not really for the car (see driveway, below). Instead, this necessary space, with blue up-and-over door, is somewhere to keep the camping equipment, bicycles, tennis racquets, weights, ab crunchers, exercise balls and so on. Plus, of course, the chest freezer, which is stuffed with chilli, bolognese and other mince-based meals you have divided into portions and stored in Tupperware containers.

2. Macrame plant holders

For displaying your bohemian side within the respectable confines of a plant holder.
Also includes plant stands, which you understand now are a status symbol, because to have one means you've got so much space you can give over a whole corner of a room to a fern.

3. A driveway

Ideally gravel and U-shaped, because you grew up thinking that was posh and it's hard to rid yourself of this image. If you have to manoeuvre out of your driveway, it's clearly not big enough.

4. A big American-style fridge, with double doors and an ice machine

With the contents all perfectly organized and visible as soon as you open the door. There's something appealing about having your Coke cans perfectly aligned, all OCD style, in the way that David Beckham apparently does, even though you don't really drink Coke.

5. A Thermomix

You're not entirely sure what you'd do with this, nor why they cost £885, but you accidentally stumbled across one being advertised on QVC and now you want one.

Also includes: the Vitamix, the Nutribullet, or any other overpriced blender.

6. Easy access to a tennis club

Not golf, obviously – you're not that bad – but you quite like the idea of being a wholesome, sporty family that has somewhere to go on Sundays.

7. An organized garden shed

With the electric mower hanging up beside the spades and carpet tiles on the floor. Not the shed that you actually have, which has nettles growing inside it and is piled with old paint tins and rusty bicycles that fall on you the minute you open the door.

8. A carpeted bathroom

With the carpet going up the side of the bath. All these modern wooden shower mats and cold tiled floors might look hip and urban, but they feel like prison underfoot. You can't help remembering how a lovely bit of carpet enabled a soft journey from your Badedas bath to the bedroom, and your waiting powder puff.

9. A downstairs toilet with a shell-shaped loo-roll holder

Oh, for a downstairs! Oh, for a loo! Oh, for a golden shell-shaped loo-roll holder! This symbol of your success not only camouflages the toilet paper (because no one wants to think about what *that's* for), it also tricks your guests into believing they're in Atlantis, not the downstairs crapper.

10. Fitted mirrored wardrobes

Massive ones, that glide silently across the width of the whole room and which, your older children suspect, you may also have embarrassing marital sex in front of.

11. Sun loungers with cushions and an electric awning

Every year you price up proper garden furniture and every year you can't believe it's over a grand, even at Homebase. And if you want all that lounge-bed stuff you get in swanky Ibizan hotels, it's three times that. How can this be?

12. A range cooker/Aga

On which to prepare kitchen sups and hang the padded oven gloves with the French cockerel motif.

13. A dining room (or study, or conservatory, or sunroom)

Or any other room that's surplus to requirements and is just for sitting in, doing nothing. HA.

Changing your scene:
Bye-bye liberty, hello leisure centre

THEN	NOW
Writing off a Saturday because you got in at 5 a.m.	Having Saturday written off because the kids get up at 5 a.m., *even at the weekend.*
Finding yourself huddled with two friends inside a toilet cubicle.	Finding yourself huddled alone in a toilet cubicle, trying to hand-pump your engorged boobs.
Popping into town on a Saturday afternoon because you've a party that night and need something to wear.	Spending Saturday afternoon ferrying your kids to and from their parties.
Knowing every bar and restaurant in your local area.	Pressing your nose to the window of another new opening you'll never go to.
Eating out because you're too lazy to do anything else, and what else are you going to spend your money on?	Eating fish-finger sandwiches at 5 p.m. with your kids.

Having bathroom shelves heaving with expensive creams and perfumes.	Having bathroom shelves heaving with athlete's foot cream, fungal-nail treatment and Imedeen.
Fantasizing about bedding George Clooney.	Fantasizing about Anthropologie bedding.
Blowing your pay cheque on shoes.	Blowing your pay cheque on your kids' shoes, which cost *how much?*
Going to the doctor once a year for the morning-after pill.	Going to the doctor every week because your child has another rash or temperature.
Having membership at Virgin Active.	Having membership at Monkey Bizness or Gambado or whatever minging soft-play centre is local to you.
Going on holiday with friends because you like them.	Going on holiday with friends because they've got kids the right age.
Waking up with a handsome stranger in your bed.	Waking up with a snotty toddler in your face.
Not remembering going to bed last night.	Remembering every detail of the night because you were awake for all of it.

Being Too Middle Class

Pretending it was their decision to learn the cello

There's a part of you that always regrets giving up the piano. Sure, the LSO was never going to be beating down your door, but it would be nice to have a party piece – to be able to knock out Bach's Air on a G String whenever the urge took you. There's something to be said about being accomplished, like an eighteenth-century gentlewoman.

But, when you think back, you were hopeless, torturing your family with bashed-out, one-handed versions of 'Froggy Went A-Courting' and pulling any trick you could to avoid having to practise. When, finally, the teacher told your parents they were wasting their money, she wasn't wrong. You quit, and everybody involved heaved a sigh of relief.

Not that this experience stops you foisting an instrument on your own child, in some weird, cycle of abuse-type scenario. Learning an instrument is important, you tell yourself, even though 98 per cent of the population seems to get by without doing any such thing.

But perhaps that's exactly why it's important. After all, who do you know who can play the flute? Next to no one.

It's the sort of trick that marks you out from the crowd. And you quite fancy having a little Von Trapp you can wheel out at parties, while you make bad jokes about how you don't know where he gets it from. If it wins him a scholarship to some posho school – well, so much the better. Besides, if he sticks with it, who knows where it could lead? If nothing else, it'll be something to put on his Tinder profile.

And how cute he looks lugging around that tuba, you think – like some innocent 1950s schoolboy parachuted into the modern world. That's what you see, anyway. What the other parents see is a stressed, over-scheduled child being pushed by his hideous tiger mother into fulfilling her dreams. Some give you backhanded compliments about how young he is; others just give you sidelong glances in the playground. Either way, short of making him spend the holidays doing Kumon maths and Mandarin, there's nothing more you could do to mark yourself out as a monstrous pushy parent.

So you have to make up some story about how it was all his idea to take it up. 'He saw his big sister playing and was desperate to join in,' you tell people. 'We said he was too young, but when he started picking up twigs in the park and pretending to play the violin, we finally relented.'

'And how's he getting on with it?' they ask, playing along with the charade. Because, while one half of them is judging you like mad, the other half is now panicking that they haven't got their own kid into music lessons and have killed her life chances.

At this point you decide not to mention the blackmail and begging, that you've given up entirely on making him practise and consider it a win if he even gets to the lesson. You can't say any of this as it merely confirms their belief that you are horrible, and that your child should be playing outside and having an actual childhood, instead of being cooped up indoors learning scales on a sunny afternoon.

And a part of you thinks they are right. After all, you know exactly where all this is leading, and it isn't Carnegie Hall. Why not save yourself the hassle and quit now? But you would then have to explain to the teacher that he hates it, which is kind of awkward when she made such a big thing of how he's finally managing to stand in the right position.

And what if he does have some tiny kernel of talent waiting to reveal itself? If he doesn't play an instrument now, he's unlikely to do so ever again in his life. This is your child's only real chance to discover a passion for music – who are you to deprive him of that opportunity? So you continue with the rigmarole, which for him is a grind and for you is Yet Another Thing You've Got To Turn Up To. Until one day, with any luck, his teacher tells you that you're wasting your money.

Forcing cultural experiences on them because you want to visit the shop

As much as you like to think you enjoy going to museums and exhibitions, it's always a pleasant surprise when you walk through to what you think is another gallery, only to find that it's the end and you're at the shop.

Because there's something about museum shops, with their carefully curated selection of arty prints and post-cards, novelty stationery and jewellery your mum would like, that makes them ideal for browsing. This isn't your common-or-garden-variety consumerism – you're not at Lakeside now, uh-uh. It's shopping you can feel good about. This is *art*. Many of the items on display you'd struggle to find elsewhere. And even though you're not planning to buy any of them – have you seen the prices? – it's nice to have a gander and see what educational-yet-stylish toy you would buy your son were you inclined to spend thirty quid on him that day.

Sometimes you even find that the less appealing the museum, the better the shop. It's as if the big cheeses at the London Transport Museum know that most mothers would rather cook their own insides than spend the after-noon learning about buses, and so compensate by making the shop a bona-fide draw. Here you'll find a vast archive of vintage travel posters, along with station clocks, lug-gage racks and cushions *in the exact same fabric as you get on the Tube*. Meanwhile, the Design Museum is, for the most part, a meh collection of everyday items you're already familiar with. But what a shop! There's no better place to buy a child's present that tells the parents how clever and thoughtful you are. Same goes for the V&A Museum of Childhood. It's some old toys really, isn't it, if we're hon-est? But the shop! Etc.

But museums are not all about the shop. There's usu-ally a cafe, too, with proper coffee and homemade scones. Unlike most regular cafes, which seem to have colluded and decided that what will keep today's toddler happy is a few coloured pencils and a paper menu, museum cafes give you an airy room, space to park the buggy and properly kid-friendly food. And what with all those tourist groups and school trips, the atmosphere is usually chaotic enough that no one's going to notice if your child's using the cutlery to play a drum solo on the table.

This makes a change from most cafes, where you are quickly reminded that, in this country, children are tolerated in the same way as, say, pigeons. Nobody complains outright, but someone usually makes it clear that you are committing the sin of being Mum with a Buggy. Meanwhile your child ignores the pasta pomodoro you have spent £6 on and makes a break from the high chair, only to throw a tantrum because you won't let him go in the kitchen. Once your baby becomes a toddler, there are only so many experiences like this you can endure before you admit that you and cafes need to take a break from each other.

But you miss them while you hang out in soft plays, libraries and parks. It isn't long before you find yourself aching to go somewhere that's geared towards adults, where your senses aren't pummelled by primary-coloured murals and 100-decibel screams.

That's why the art gallery or museum can be such a life-changer. Strictly speaking, your toddler might not be old enough for the kids' trails and treasure hunts these places like to lay on. And maybe, if you're honest, your child isn't that interested in English regional chairs of the eighteenth century or Alexander Rodchenko's avant-garde photography. But that makes two of you.

And who's to say that your child won't get anything out

of the experience? Because what is a museum or gallery but a big space? And what do toddlers need to burn off all that excess energy? Ex*actly*. Here you have a huge indoor space, where children are, if not welcomed, then accepted as part of the deal, and that doesn't look like it was decorated by SpongeBob SquarePants. On a quiet weekday it's all rather civilized. If everything goes to plan, you get to feel like you're being an involved, hands-on mother *and* exercising your brain. Well done, you.

So what if you don't get to see anything because your daughter's too busy bombing it down the corridors and trying to climb the stairs? Yes, it's embarrassing when the security guard tells you off because she's limboed the rope and is trying to high-five a Rembrandt. But you can reassure yourself that the staff have seen worse. They must have done. Surely.

The more ambitious mother can tell herself that if she immerses her toddler in culture, something will surely go in. It's easy to kid yourself that your son will soak up the atmosphere and grow up feeling comfortable in highfalutin' places, unintimidated by high art. In years to come, when he paints his bedroom black, you can say proudly, 'Well, of course, he grew up seeing the Rothkos at Tate Modern.'

But it doesn't have to be Tate Modern, or any other world-class attraction. Let's face it, it could be the museum devoted to Allen keys and you wouldn't mind. On holiday you find yourself drawn to honey farms and waxwork museums, manor houses and arboretums – anywhere, as long as there's somewhere you can grab an Earl Grey and have a squiz at the nice tote bags in the shop.

Bribing your children in restaurants

In the same way that people who went to Oxbridge always tell you as much within ten minutes of meeting them, so the parents of good eaters like to share that their offspring loves pad thai, or sashimi, or some other dish unlikely to make it on to the Wacky Warehouse kids' menu any time soon. More infuriatingly, they take the credit for it, saying things like, 'Well, we just exposed him to everything when he was really young,' as if you only offered your child crackers and Rice Krispies for eighteen months.

Because every parent wants a good eater. Not a fatty (there can be a fine line), but someone who gratefully hoovers up their supper every night, and saves you that whole panic about whether they're getting enough iron and vitamin D. Or, worse still, having to give the shepherd's pie – the one you gave a face made from tomato and red pepper, like Annabel Karmel told you to – to the dog.

And thinking of new and interesting things to feed them, day after day, week after week, is hard enough, without having a little prince or princess who doesn't eat pizza, or fish fingers, or any of the other key food groups. Anyone who's experienced the frustration of trying to get a child to eat will know that, in terms of stress, it's up there with hostage negotiation. The annoying thing is that it shouldn't be difficult. The simple answer is to starve them until they eat anything you put in front of them, or so your dad keeps telling you. But somehow it never works like that, and what you end up with is a child who lives on toast and bananas.

Mind you, even though you've likely been through it yourself, that doesn't stop you doing an inward eye roll when faced with someone else's picky kid. Then you can't help but feel smug when yours wolf down your fish pie (which they are now conditioned to like), while the other kid whines something about only liking the other kind of potato. This child will forever be a bit wet in your eyes, whereas the kid who eats your cooking and asks for seconds is sent from heaven.

Naturally you want other parents to think this highly of your child. So in your bid to create a good eater – and because you can't be arsed to make any more shepherd's pies with faces on them *in individual ramekins* (thank you, Annabel Karmel), you try taking them to restaurants.

Admittedly there are ulterior motives at work here – you want to go to a restaurant! – but there are ways of selling the idea to yourself. Perhaps restaurant-quality food is what's missing from their diet. After all, when you read interviews with chefs, they're always referring to family meals out where they order plates of fritto misto and arancini, and the kids enthusiastically help themselves. Maybe this is where you're going wrong, you think. You're not ordering enough fried octopus in restaurants.

So you try going out to eat. Maybe not full-on ethnic, not first time around, anyway, but something that way inclined – somewhere exotic that's westernized enough for everyone to feel that they're on safe territory. You're thinking Wagamama or maybe Wahaca. Somewhere that does a kids' menu that isn't five variations of beans and chips.

This will hopefully expand their food repertoire, but also gives you the chance to get them used to eating out. Because behaving well in restaurants is considered a sign of sophistication in children. That French children are reputed to behave themselves in restaurants is a key part of their carefully crafted image as World's Best-Behaved Children. Your city friends talk about their rural nieces and nephews using words like 'noisy' and 'feral'. 'They've got no idea how to behave in restaurants,' they say, to illustrate their point.

And nor have your kids, it turns out. You spend the whole meal trying to bribe them with the prospect of ice cream. 'Eat your dinner and you can have an ice cream.' 'Throw that spoon one more time and you won't get an ice cream.' Your meal becomes a race against the clock as you try to persuade the waitress to bring this bloody ice cream before the kids are out of their chairs and making a break for the exit. You neck your wine and skip the coffees as you realize you are on borrowed time before they get bored of your iPhone (OK, you cheated) and holler the place down.

And really it would have been a nicer – and cheaper – experience for everybody if you'd simply made spag bol at home. But you do that every night and it's boring. And you want your child to be that kid who eats pad thai and sashimi, goddammit.

The lies we tell

When someone asks how you are, you never actually tell them. If you bump into a dad from school in Sainsbury's and he says, 'Hey, how you doing?', you'd never say, 'I think I've just come on and I'm worried the blood is going to leak through my new jeans any second now, so can you stop talking to me because I've got to get to the car and I totally don't fancy you anyway.' You say, 'Yeah, good, thanks! Glad it's nearly the end of term though, aren't you? There are some very tired little people in our house!' and other boring platitudes about him getting together for a boys' night with your other half.

We all keep a box of lies handy, so no one knows we're crying inside. Here are a few of the most common ones:

What We Say	What We Mean
Yeah, they get on really well.	They fight and hit each other from the moment they wake up. Every day. It's exhausting. Sometimes I shout at them to stop it so loudly, I think I need restraining.
Izzy had such a lovely time at your house, thank you so much for having her, she hasn't stopped talking about it.	She hasn't said anything about it. Actually, I haven't even asked her.

He'll eat pretty much anything. Yeah, he loves fish.	He eats pizza and Wotsits. He will leave anything else you offer him.
They played really nicely. Josh is very confident, isn't he?	Your child is a little shit and a bully, and I'm never inviting him over ever again.
We must get together without the children one day and have a proper catch-up.	I literally can't think of anyone I'd rather hang out with less than you. Please never let me be left alone in a room with you and your Joules fleece.
He stopped crying as soon as you left.	The whey-faced brat didn't stop moaning all day.
She's so like you.	Are you sure they gave you the right one?
Noah thought your present was really great. Thank you.	All the presents ended up in a huge, tagless pile. I have no idea who bought what. Did you even get him anything? Am I making an arse of myself by thanking you here?
They hardly watch any telly. I'll put it on if I'm cooking, or in the shower, but nothing much apart from that.	The only time they are not watching telly is when they are asleep.
It gets easier.	When you start taking anti-depressants.

The Gates of Hell: Back to School

Over-promising at the PTA

Starting at a new school can be as harrowing for a mother as it can for any child. Children, after all, can wee in their pants and hit the other kids if they feel lonely at their new school. No such venting of the emotions is permitted for their mothers, who have to stand there like a cretin every day in the playground, waiting for their kid to come out clutching yet another picture made of leaves.

It is these feelings of vulnerability that make many of us sign up to the PTA as soon as we join a new school. Like a cult preying on unhinged teenage girls, the PTA appears to offer a lifeline to the disenfranchised new mother. 'Whatever you can give' is all that's required in terms of your time. In return you'll receive an instant way in, and people to wave at in the playground. You'll look as if you belong. You also think to yourself, as if no one had thought of it before, that joining the PTA will give you some guaranteed prestige among the teachers. They will think you are an amazing woman because of all the support you are giving them, and treat your child accordingly, with special attention and extra gold stars.

Besides, how hard can it be, running the hot-chocolate stall at the school fireworks fundraiser? This is you, who used to run brand-focus workshops for company CEOs. You used to advise people to do things like 'keep your powder dry' and talk about ideas being your 'currency'. You were a fully paid-up career wanker. Pass the squirty cream and let's show these PTA motherfuckers how it's done!

What you hadn't taken into account was how shit you've become at managing your time these days. Or maybe it's just that you don't *have* any time these days. You can't be sure. What's the time? Either way, when you were running those workshops from your office with the Eames chairs, with your mini Danish pastries and free-flowing San Pellegrino, there wasn't a whining preschooler at your feet and you didn't have to stop what you were doing at 2.30 p.m. every day to go and pick up the child with all the pictures of leaves. You didn't have to do the shopping and cook the tea and wash the pooey pants and talk to Wessex Water for seven hours either. Your can-do approach to your career was allowed to flourish, because it existed in glorious isolation, hermetically sealed in an air-conditioned space devoted to the cultivation of your cerebral powers.

Volunteering to get sponsorship from local businesses for the fireworks bonanza sounded like a piece of piss when you stupidly said you would do it. But now it weighs heavy on your mind, keeping you awake at night and giving you panic attacks. In your head you constructed a sophisticated sponsorship package, presented with fancy graphs and figures in a little folder, delivered by hand to your carefully targeted list of local businesses. In reality you haven't managed to find anyone's number and you're hoping your mate's husband who's a builder will cough up the £500 you said you could raise no problem.

And you wish you hadn't agreed to do that as well as bake a load of cakes and make a ton of jolly jars (whatever they are), and write the fun quiz and generally do everything. In fact, come to think of it, who else is actually doing anything on this PTA?

Come to think of it again, your strategy of ingratiating yourself (ergo your child) with the teachers doesn't seem to be working. Not one of them thanked you for your superior lemon drizzle, and at parents' evening you got rushed through just like everyone else, after being told your kid seemed to be 'doing fine'. Where was the special treatment? Did his teacher even know you were on the PTA?

Slowly it dawns on you that the PTA is not a bunch of lovely mums all 'leaning in' for the greater good (and some grace and favour from the teachers). It's a sinking ship, like the one in *Pirates of the Caribbean*, where all the pirates are in fact ghosts. It's a group of women with good intentions, but no actual time, feeling over-stretched and over-obliged. A bit like the WI or the Masons – an institution rooted in another era, when men won the bread and the women baked it.

You realize the teachers are too overwrought and stressed trying to write progress trackers and reading records and generally control the chaos to give a shit about your cakes. They can barely remember your child's name, never mind give him special treatment.

And you wonder why it's only the mothers who seem to join the PTA, even though most of them are working and looking after kids and clearly don't have the time for this stuff. Why do we feel it's our duty to add another burden to the load? Why does it never occur to the men to find the time? Why did I ever join the PTA? WHY? And you get so angry thinking about it that you spill the food colouring in the icing and completely ruin your lemon drizzle.

Not coping with the school holidays

Mothers of school-aged kids tend to fall into two camps: those who look forward to the end of term because they get to see more of their children, and the ones for whom the holidays mean one thing: ball ache.

When the kids are small, people talk of the magical watershed moment: *starting school*. You can get your life back, they say, have time to yourself at last. Briefly, you allow yourself to imagine a new Hush-catalogue existence of part-time work, kundalini yoga and flat whites with beautiful friends. But like so many of the platitudes people spout about parenthood, this is bollocks. Because no one mentions the 50 per cent of the year they are not at school at all. They are on holiday. At home. With nothing to do.

Terms – all three of them – last about ten weeks, and whizz past in a blur of late arrivals, after-school clubs and rank PTA cake sales. And you are just finding the beat – remembering recorder on Monday and swimming on

Friday, bring a snack on Wednesday because they go straight to Beavers, take Gemma home for Janey on Thursday and don't forget her book bag – you are beginning to nail this school shizzle, when term ends. And you are left hanging, suspended in motion, like Wile E. Coyote when the road disappears from under him, before he falls into the canyon below.

Because the holidays are exactly that – holes. Vast, empty wastelands of unpunctuated time. Days without beginnings and ends. Weeks without routines or schedules. In summer, there are consecutive *months* of it. During these stretches, you're reminded of what life was like before they went to school. It's just you and them. For the whole day. Only this time round they don't have a sleep after lunch and can't be fooled into believing that a trip to Morrisons is fun. They want entertainment, things to do: play dates and sleepovers. They are demanding and expensive and, worst of all, bored.

Summer is most traumatic by far. Faced with a full six weeks of your new reality, you scratch around for holiday clubs and sports camps, and turn up to any old activity in any old village hall if it will pass a few hours and keep your house marginally less scruffy. You sign them up for things you know they'll hate and may possibly find distressing, telling yourself and them that it's your job to broaden their horizons. Really, it's to give yourself a break. Or, more accurately, time to work and/or clean the house. Both of which feel like a luxury escape after three days of the holidays.

And it's true, a few days with the cult of Stagecoach can pass the time productively. Summer-holiday workshop?

Ten till three for five whole days? I'll take that. So good for their confidence. But you spend so long on the admin, travel, packed lunches and kit required (don't forget to buy your jazz shoes, everybody!), you wonder if it's not more hassle than it's worth. And, since you ask, it's worth about £300 for two kids for the week. Which would probably pay for you all to go to Menorca for a week on a last-minute deal. If you could only find a minute, last or otherwise, to look for one online.

It's around now that you remember you didn't do all these expensive activities when you were a kid. They can play in the garden in a paddling pool! They can visit nearby places of interest! They can do crafts, like this fun make-your-own-kaleidoscope kit. But you have made the error of not leaving the house yet, so have lost them to their screens. They are with Minecraft and Crossy Roads now. And the house is quiet. And you know you should be opposed to this, seeing as how it's 32 degrees outside and they're in the lounge with the curtains closed at 10.30 a.m. But you like the peace too much to disrupt them. Besides, they need some downtime. They're so busy. It's nice for them not to be rushing somewhere. You repeat this mantra until September, and make them promise to say they had a staycation if anyone asks.

Though shorter, half-term can be equally vicious. Half-term uses the element of surprise to stun working parents, appearing out of nowhere, often during the most dismal weather of the year. Half-term also comes with an arsenal of add-on tortures, such as Halloween and Pancake Day. These 'festivals' mean that, as well as looking after your kids for a week in the rain, you have to embrace activities based entirely on the consumption of sugar. But of all the half-terms, February is the cruellest. You've barely recovered from the horrors of Christmas. You've still got the bad clothes from Monsoon you were given, no chance of a refund now. Over-exposure to radiators and alcohol has given you the complexion of a lizard. You've been wearing the same grey jumper since September. You've battled through the disappointment of Valentine's Day (post received: one leaflet from Relate). And, to top it all, everyone else seems to be going skiing. If you're not going skiing, there is little for your children to do during this bleakest of weeks, besides binging on Haribo and watching TV.

All of which makes you nostalgic for the best holiday of all – Christmas. Once the presents/cooking/slavery bit is over, this is the only true holiday in the calendar. Because this is when you can legitimately allow the kids to stay inside eating Heroes and wearing onesies for two weeks, when the only reading challenge they have is the *Radio Times*. And when someone asks them what they did in the holidays, they can tell the truth. Because that's exactly what they were supposed to be doing.

Fancying the only male teacher at school

It's probably just natural selection in action, this crush you have on that teacher at school. You used to do it at work, too – plump for the best of a bad bunch. Had you ever encountered your overweight boss with a penchant for lilac shirts in a bar or club, it's unlikely you'd have been that dreamy about him. But in the gated community of the office, where his biggest competition was the guy who ate McDonald's at his desk and then went to the lav with a copy of the *Mail* – well, compared to him, Lilac Shirt was smokin'.

Something similar seems to happen to you at your kids' school. Only it's intensified now, thanks to a lack of significant rivals. Mr Whatsisface is pretty much the only man for miles. You'd heard there was a shortage of male teachers in primary schools. You knew they were offering golden handshakes and the like to entice young men into teaching. But you didn't think things were this bad. There are literally no men here. It's like the War. Have we thought about shipping some over from America, maybe?

It doesn't help that you're older, and experiencing the famous 'sexual peak' of a woman in her late thirties and early forties (see also: Fancying younger men, p. 70). You understand now what this actually means – that you spend life in a state of imaginary rumpy-pumpy with pretty much every man you encounter who isn't your partner. You are beginning to have some small understanding of what it feels like to be a man. In this sense, Mr Whatsisname is just another notch on your towering, but hypothetical, sexual-peak bedpost.

But the context is potent, too. The school environment is laced with so much sexual undertone, it's hard to believe teachers get any work done in these places. All that discipline and correction; all those stationery cupboards and bike sheds. In the assemblies that parents are allowed to watch, you sit and study them all intensely. Wonder which one's a lesbian. Who has the best threads. I bet she likes a drink. And just look at Mr Whatsisface, he's very authoritative. He's taking no bullshit from those six-year-olds. So powerful.

So the guy stands no chance, really. Whether he's genuinely buff, straight out of college and all I-want-to-make-a-difference, or cynical and bored and completely past his sell-by, he takes on magical qualities now that he's kind of the only man you see regularly. Other than your husband and the postman, that is – and you've tried really hard to fancy him but it's just not happening.

Not only that, here is a significant male authority figure in your child's life. Is your sexual desire for him rooted in some visceral, primeval urge to align yourself with the alphas of the pack? Should something happen to your beloved when he's a-hunting in the forest, would this fine, upstanding specimen with all the brain cells be a good replacement to help you rear your young?

Lord knows. But you're definitely thinking a bit harder about what to wear for the school run. It's OK to wear heels on a rainy Monday morning, right? And nothing wrong with a push-up bra at pick-up time, is there? You become uncharacteristically helpful and interested in all matters educational. Are any mums available to walk with the children to the leisure centre on Tuesday? Why, yes, I'd be happy to. I just love helping children, and leisure centres. You want someone to come in and listen to them reading? Of course. I love sitting in corridors listening to kids who aren't even mine reading really slowly.

You construct elaborate fantasies about finding yourself alone with the victim. If he's the head (aiming high – you go, girl), it's usually in his office, after school. He's asked for your input on the school's five-year plan and, you know, one thing leads to another. If he's a form teacher, you wonder if perhaps you might share a car journey on a school trip one day. Break down on the way home from Bristol Zoo, say. Stuck in a lay-by for hours with only some sandwiches and a can of warm 7 Up. It's hot and something about being in the car invites an intimacy that takes you both by surprise . . .

You have a big old schoolgirl crush, and you're behaving like a proper eejit. Hopefully this too shall pass before you do anything stupid and find you've eloped to Wales with your son's twenty-three-year-old teacher. Maybe another alpha male joins the staff and diverts your gaze in assembly. Or you go back to work and lilac-shirt man makes a comeback. Closer to the truth, you find you are getting nowhere with Mr Whatsisface. It's as if it's happened to him before, mums crushing on him like this. And although it's kind of frustrating not to bag the prize, you also can't help feeling relieved to wear comfortable shoes for the school run again.

Feeling like a fraud at school

Unless you're a teacher, or dinner lady, you probably haven't spent much time in a school since that day in 1993 when you got your A-level results, and thought it was really hardcore to smoke outside the head's office window so that she could see you.

Stepping back inside the institution, with its cabbage-and-mashed-potato smell, munchkin-sized toilets and corridors lined with posters about the Romans, it can be hard to believe you're now the parent and not the child. And since you don't really believe it yourself, you wonder if other people here might not believe it either. You feel like a fraud. Here are some of the signs:

- You put on a posh, exaggerated mum voice when you phone in to say your kid is ill.
- You're not quite sure how to introduce yourself on the phone. Do you use your actual name? Or are you so-and-so's mum? Will they even know who you're talking about?
- Instead of saying you overslept/forgot/lost it, you make up excuses for being late/not bringing in the permission slip/PE kit: It was the traffic/ my husband lost the slip/I think someone stole it.
- Part of you wants to volunteer to help with reading, school trips, etc., but the other part – the dominant part, it turns out – wants to skive off and do nothing of the sort.
- You're a bit starry-eyed about the head and behave like a teenage groupie around her, laughing too hard at her jokes and telling lies about how much your child is loving school.
- In an effort to fit in, you try to be friends with everyone and go over the top with smiling and seeming like the nicest mum in the world.
- You feel clueless about the school routine – who teaches what, and where your kids should be at what time. But are too afraid to ask anyone for help.

- Even now, twenty years later, you switch off in assembly and still can't decide if it's uncool to join in with the Lord's Prayer/singing the hymns.
- You feel like you've done something wrong from the moment you set foot on school grounds, and wear an expression of mild terror whenever you see a teacher.
- You can't escape the feeling that you're about to be bollocked.

World Book Day, and other ways to torment mothers

It's not like they didn't have fancy dress when you were a kid. You can still remember your disappointment, at the Brownies' end-of-year party, as the other girls got to go as Snow White and Tinkerbell, Betty Rubble and Alice, while your parents stuck you in a massive cardboard box and said you were a present. So they definitely had fancy dress. They just didn't have quite so much of it, was all.

You don't remember the school colluding in it, either. Apart from the occasional trip, when you'd all get madly over-excited about the prospect of going to Longbridge in your civvies, there was no call to wear anything other than your uniform, an outfit designed to take the effort out of dressing for school.

But not content with making you read about the interminable adventures of Biff and Kipper, and collect mountains of packaging for junk modelling, your son's school now sends home a breezy-as-you-like letter telling you that World Book Day is coming up, and – to celebrate

– could you just knock up a costume based on your child's favourite literary character?

Favourite literary character? You weren't aware he had one. Oh God, you think. This is one of those occasions where you've got to pretend he loves Beatrix Potter and A. A. Milne to save face, when you know for a fact he'd rather read the Argos catalogue.

Your immediate thought is how to make this easy on yourself (you are your parents' child, after all). And if you have a philosophy on parenting, it's that you should do with them the things you're good at (in your case: reading, going to the cinema) and farm out the rest to other people. And sewing costumes is up there with playing shops and sitting patiently through song-and-dance recitals on the list of things that you are not good at. But it turns out you're in luck, because H&M is way ahead of you on the costume-making front. And graphic novels count, right?

Certainly, your son agrees, and only wants to go as Spiderman. But then you start seeing various articles about World Book Day, which describe the lengths to which mothers go to reproduce hand-stitched Hagrid and Cat in the Hat outfits, and have an about-turn. You decide that shop-bought superhero costumes are a cheat too far. You're not aware that anyone has sent out a list of rules, but for some reason you feel obliged to make your own.

'Spiderman doesn't count.'

'But Ciaran at school's got a book about superheroes, and it's got Spiderman in it.'

'Still doesn't count.'

'I hate you.'

It gets more heated than this, when you force him into a knight costume – which seems somehow more acceptable than a superhero, what with its historical references – until he kills it by skipping around the room, singing, 'I'm Mike the Knight!'

What follows turns out to be one of those entirely unnecessary rows that come about as a result of the pressure mothers put themselves under to appear, if not perfect, then better at this than they really are. It's the same instinct that makes them go to music-and-movement classes nobody enjoys, and provide carrot batons they know no one will eat at parties. When it comes to maintaining appearances, most mothers are up there with Hyacinth Bouquet. But while society likes to blame mothers for turning parenthood into a competition, it never takes into account the fact that it keeps throwing goals and challenges at them. Make a costume! Bake biscuits! Sew name tags on everything that isn't locked down! Motherhood can end up feeling like a game show, only without the promise of a new dishwasher at the end of it.

Your Facebook feed tells you that you're not the only one feeling the tyranny of World Book Day, either. Your friends seem to fall neatly into two camps: the ones who post status updates reading, 'World Book Day? What fresh hell is this?? Why did nobody tell me?!' and the ones who've been up all night fashioning red wool into Pippi Longstocking plaits.

You have to admire this latter group, and maybe feel a pang of guilt for not being on board with them. But costume making is one of those activities you're not sure comes with a big enough payback to make it worth your while. It's the same reason that, come their birthday, you're reluctant to spend two days recreating the Millennium Falcon in fondant icing. Because if you're going to invest that much time and energy into something, there has to be a sufficient reward attached. And that needs to be more than a bunch of five-year-old ingrates stuffing their face with it. No, if you're going to put that much of your heart and soul into a cake, you want it preserved and displayed on a plinth, for everyone to admire for ever.

The same goes for their World Book Day costume. Sure, you get a photo out of it. But, really, after the initial, 'Oh, you're Wally from *Where's Wally?!*' what's in it for you? Surely the creativity here lies not in creating an elaborate costume, but in thinking of one that involves the least effort on your part. And, after a little thought, you've got it. Put him in a massive cardboard box – he's Mr Strong.

The Definition of Madness: Doing It All Again

Short-changing the second child

You've got to feel sorry for younger children. Doomed to be bossed about by their siblings and forgotten at Christmas by the distant relatives, they also lose out on the parenting front. Because all that focus you concentrated on the first one – reading the right books, eating the right foods and generally going out of your way to produce a little Einstein – somehow goes out of the window with the second child, who's lucky if he gets his breakfast on time.

We believe there's even a name for it: second-child syndrome. Here are some common signs:

1. Forgetting that you're not supposed to drink wine and eat shellfish during pregnancy.
2. Giving up breastfeeding at the first opportunity.
3. Not taking them to baby singing/Gymboree/ Kindermusik or any other activity you tortured yourself with first time round.
4. Never taking photos of them, casting their feet

in clay, creating a memory box or filling in their baby book.

5. The first one has a personalized hooded animal towel, a wooden train that spells out his name and a pillow with his initials embroidered on it. The second one scarcely has his own toothbrush.

6. Obsessing about milestones with the first one, and then failing to notice them at all with later children.

7. Dressing them in their sibling's holey cast-offs.

8. Sending them to the shit nursery because it makes your life easier.

9. Not bothering to make friends with the other parents there.

10. Scaring them with the older sibling's choice of movies/TV.

11. Not buying them new toys, so all their puzzles and shape sorters have pieces missing, and their pop-up books have the pop-up bits ripped out.

12. Putting them in the tiny bedroom.

13. Agonizing first time round about which school will best suit your child's character, then sending all subsequent kids wherever the first one goes.

Becoming that ineffectual mother who can't control her children

Say what you like about spanking, it was an effective weapon in a mother's armoury. Whatever naughtiness our parents' generation got up to, *their* parents could always come back with, 'Do that again and you'll get a whack.' As a punishment, surely that ticked all the boxes. It was clear and unambiguous. It was harsh enough to act as a deterrent. It's unlikely they even had to hit the child – the threat would have been enough to have them haring up the stairs, holding their hands over their bottoms.

Life is so much harder now that we're not allowed to beat our children. You wouldn't mind, but no one seems to have come up with a decent alternative. There's the negotiation, where you try and discuss your child's transgression, like you're Angela Merkel and he's some errant minister. But this usually results in him looking bored and waiting for you to finish, while you wonder if you wouldn't be better off talking to the table.

Alternatively, you can pout and say in an ickle-baby voice, 'That makes Mummy sad.' But behaviour like this in a grown woman is, frankly, degrading. In any case, three-year-olds aren't known for their empathy. If anything, it only makes the situation more awkward as your son carries on whacking your friend's kid with a Stickle Brick, wearing an expression of psychopathic indifference, while your friend looks on, horrified.

Threats are useful – telling your child that he's not going to the party/swimming, etc., can be an effective tool. But unless his life is packed back-to-back with fun stuff, you may find yourself struggling to remember something – anything – you have coming up that he might conceivably be looking forward to. You're not going to school? No, that's not going to work. Violin is cancelled? Damn. From blackmail it's only a short hop to bribery, so you end up pulling from the air something that you *would* have bought him, had he not been such an arsehole. 'You won't get that Kinder Egg!' The one you then, of course, have to buy him.

Because that's the other bonus of spanking – there's no forward planning involved. You can simply shout, 'You'll get a spank!' It becomes a kind of reflex, something you say without thinking. The downside of that being that you end up looking like Popeye as you wave your fist, muttering, 'Why, I oughta . . .'

But that beats the alternative, which is where you start making your threat, only to realize you haven't actually thought of one. This leaves you stammering, 'Don't do that or I'll . . . I'll . . .' at which point you both know the battle is lost. Either that or you come out with some threat they know you'll never follow through, like giving away their toys or never letting them watch TV again. Like lions, kids sense weakness, and you are limping like a three-legged fawn.

Failing that, there's the countdown. 'I'm going to count to five,' you say. The risk here being that he lets you get to five. Because what then? You have nothing. Otherwise there's that old favourite, the naughty – sorry, the time-out step. But it doesn't take the averagely bright child long to work out that a) sitting on a step is not that terrible, and b) if they get off it and start playing, their mother is all out of threats and they've won. The same goes for, 'Get to your room,' although at least you can holler this in a satis-fyingly scary voice.

Developing an evil voice is definitely worth the effort. Quieter is better than loud; low-pitched is more effective than high. What you're looking for is somewhere between

Jeremy Irons in *The Lion King* and the demon in *The Exorcist*. But the better your evil voice, the less portable it is. What works a dream in the confines of your kitchen is going to get you looks out in public. On the other hand, now that everybody's policing each other's behaviour, you can't try any of the tricks you use at home without failing somebody's good-parent test, so you might as well not even worry about it.

The advice professionals offer is to reward good behaviour and simply ignore the bad stuff. But again, try that in public, when your child is being a thug and you are merrily oblivious, pretending to study the emergency-procedure leaflet on the wall. See how many invites to the Community Family Fun Day BBQ that gets you.

Generally, the experts are no help – they talk incessantly about the need for 'consistency'. But this doesn't take into account the fact that on some days you're going to be massively bothered by things that, on others, you're happy to let slide. Inconsistency is a parent's prerogative. Letting them stay up past 9 p.m. one night and then raging because they're not in bed by 7 p.m. the next surely comes with the turf. Fighting it is futile.

It's tough because you're supposed to be the woman whose children behave impeccably on trains and in cafes. Yet you have no punishment at your disposal that doesn't leave them laughing in your face. The result is that you become a weak leader. You become that ineffectual mother who can't control her children.

Admitting That You Love It Really

Valuing your friendships

Once the chaos of babyhood is over, you may find you emerge with a smaller network than you once had, but the good news is that the friendships you hold on to become more valuable to you than ever.

After all, it's the old friends you can phone after a two-year hiatus and know that, even if they're a bit miffed with you, they'll still be pleased to hear your voice. Or at least you don't have to worry that they won't remember you or experience that awkward moment when they say, '*So . . .*', your cue to get to the point of your call.

Admittedly, these old friendships have their downsides. Old friends love nothing better than to spoil your attempts to reinvent yourself as someone cool and sophisticated. They remember all the events you have chosen to forget and, if they ever feel you're getting too up yourself, will cheerfully remind you of that embarrassing letter you once wrote to *The Face* and that boy you snogged on the French exchange who turned out to collect trolls. All too often they have photographic evidence.

But we put them through a lot, these old friends. Our

expectations of them are high, and we feel let down by them easily. Often we demand more of them than we do the newer, shinier people we're trying to get in with, and let them get away with less. We expect them to know when we're too busy to chat, but are put out when we find they're unavailable. Likewise, we know their traits and habits, and still might not have 100 per cent forgiven them for that time they made us wait two hours in the cold because they'd met a man and no one had invented mobile phones yet.

For all its lonely moments, motherhood involves meeting a lot of new people – at NCT meetings and toddler groups, playgrounds and nursery Christmas parties. This means you spend large amounts of time having to be nice and pretend you like things you don't, so as not to appear controversial. Which is exhausting, frankly. This always makes it a treat when you see your old friends, who know and get you. You don't have to prove or explain yourself to them and, no matter how much time has gone by, can instantly bounce back to the private jokes and silly voices that amused you when you were sixteen.

You were there at their eighteenths and twenty-firsts and are still hanging around for the thirtieths and forti-eths. You know their parents and their siblings, and that their great aunt Julie decided she was a lesbian and stopped speaking to everybody. These are the women you think of when you hear that song you know they'd like or read that book that would make them laugh. They're the ones you call for a quick chat and hang up realizing it's been nearly two hours and you forgot to give the kids their tea. Or you don't speak for months but can send them one picture of a wine label, knowing they'll instantly remember what happened that night.

Funnily enough, these friends don't always make for the best anecdotes – they're often not the ones you go to the flashy places with or slave over Ottolenghi books for. But that's because you can be honest with them about being broke, and spending a lot of money feels like a waste because you know you'll have just as nice a time over a bowl of pasta in your pyjamas. Which your new friends might find a bit of a weird invite.

And over that pasta you'll get the complete, unabridged version of what they've been up to, and vice versa. New friends tend to get the nice, pre-watershed episode, while old friends get the Adult Channel-edit. This is more polite somehow. These newer relationships are too fresh to reveal your full-blown craziness – you don't want to scare them off just yet.

But the unedited stories are far more satisfying. After all, these days the gossip is pretty juicy, as you find yourselves going through some proper, grown-up shit – affairs and divorces, illness and debt. In other hands, this subject matter could be bleak, but even in the direst of situations you laugh. You realize that, as nice as those new friends are, they just don't make you belly laugh in the way that your old friends can. And when it comes to offering advice, only your old friends can give you a fully rounded picture, because they know that you've always picked the wrong men, and have never been able to hold on to money.

Sadly, these older friends have an unfortunate habit of living miles away, which is a pain, but gives you a nice excuse to visit their part of the world. You feel comfortable enough in their house to make your own coffee and don't panic if you finish the milk. These visits also mean you get to spend proper time with them, with breakfast and the papers and a long afternoon, rather than a quick two courses and you're out.

When it comes to parenting, meanwhile, these are the friends you can drop your guard with – the ones with whom you can skip the pretence that you're aceing this motherhood thing. They don't care if you buy all the kids' clothes from Boden and all their food at Planet Organic. In fact, they think you're mad if you do. Friends like this are a gift for your children too – they're the extended network they grow up with, the family friends you know will always be on their side. They're the women your children would call 'aunty' if anyone actually wanted to be called aunty any more. Your kids describe each other as cousins and no one ever corrects them.

It's a shame, then, that at this stage of life our friends can get a raw deal. With them there are no anniversaries, no yearly excuses to celebrate your relationship. The weekends away you once did without a thought are now mammoth events requiring three months' planning and professional admin skills. Our oldest and dearest must accept the fact that family has to come first, and all too often they'll be blown out for some child's swimming practice or in-law visit. They're rarely the people you spend Christmas with, even though you'd rather you did.

Every so often you'd like to give them a little shout-out, but that would feel a bit lame. So you carry on never quite getting round to calling them, but looking forward to the moment when you do.

When being a mother is quite good, actually

Being a mum can be so hard, it's easy to become a massive moany-pants about it. Sometimes you may even forget the perks. These include:

- Finally being able to watch the Pixar movies, read *Harry Potter* and visit Winter Wonderland without looking like the kind of woman who covers her bed with cuddly toys.
- Getting to reacquaint yourself with the toys of your own childhood (the Fisher-Price cash register, Hungry Hippos, Swingball) and then tut about how the new versions aren't nearly as good as the old ones.
- Going to cheesy restaurants, like the Hard Rock Cafe, without having to be knowing and ironic about it.
- Other passengers audibly groaning when you board the plane, but the cabin crew being really, really nice to you.
- When you're out and about and need a wee, walking into any restaurant or cafe, no matter how fancy, and saying, 'Do you mind? He's desperate, sorry.'
- Getting to park near the supermarket entrance. (OK, so it's not much of a perk, but on the bad days it's something.)
- Mother's Day, with its daffodils and breakfast in bed, handmade cards and unappetizing Rice-Krispie cakes. Not to be confused with Father's

Day, which everyone knows is commercialized American rubbish.

And then there are moments that will thaw the icy hearts of even the most sleep-deprived hags among us. These are the reasons we don't send them back. Here, in association with Hallmark, we bring you some of the best:

- When they automatically hold your hand walking down the street. This never fails to bring on the swoons. Especially good when it's a nine-year-old boy, who has momentarily forgotten how embarrassing you are.
- When they say something genuinely hilarious that makes you burst out laughing – not at them because they're cute, but with them because they're funny. You made a funny person!
- When you successfully pass a family tradition down the generations. Such as pillowcases instead of stockings at Christmas. And hard-boiled egg mashed up in a cup as a snack. This invokes a pleasing sense of all-is-well. (Doesn't work with your partner's weird traditions, like making them wait until after lunch for presents on Christmas Day, or diluting the washing-up liquid to make it last longer. Stop that.)
- When you're watching their school assembly and they win a certificate for amazing reading/scoring a goal/being nice. Here is proof, ladies and gentlemen, of your incredible parenting. The wholly narcissistic pleasure of this experience is only ever beaten by having two of your children

achieve this in the same assembly. Got three? Now you're just showing off.

- They make you find out about things it would otherwise never occur to you to question. Where do lemurs live? How close can you get to the sun without getting burnt? What's the number before infinity? Google, we owe you one.

- Every time anyone says how much like you they are. Outwardly you're like, 'Oh really? I think they're more like their dad . . .' But inside you're all like, 'Booyakasha! My genes win. Uh-huh, oh yeah,' and doing a little twerk.

- You so look forward to being without them – to be able to get on a Tube unencumbered by buggies and bags and small people who can't negotiate escalators. Then finally it happens and you go and ruin it all by missing them.

- When they want seconds of the main course (i.e. not pudding). And their friends do too. Life doesn't get any better than this. Honestly.

- When they say, 'I love you, Mummy,' apropos of nothing.

Enjoying your children

We are not supposed to wish their lives away. We should enjoy every moment, because blink and you miss it. Before you know it they've grown up and flown the nest. Childhood is so short, we should cherish every day. And all that other stuff the old people always say.

The wisdom of old people is indeed wise, but has clearly been filtered by time and buffed up with nostalgia. They've conveniently forgotten all the crap bits. Because when you're a new mum, blindly navigating the sleepless fug of the early years, it can be hard to imagine a time when you might begin to enjoy this game.

Enjoyment here is something very different from love. It's not that you don't appreciate being a mother – and them. You love them more than you imagined it was possible to love someone wearing only a nappy full of poo and a winsome smile.

Enjoying it, though, is another matter altogether. In the early years, large portions of your day – generally the awake portions – are spent doing mundane and exhausting tasks in their name: sterilizing plastic, putting Duplo back in a box 103 times, folding laundry, overseeing the brushing of teeth. You don't hesitate to do these things, because you love them, but these are not activities anyone could honestly describe as enjoyable. You understand the ominous title of that book that you can't quite get round to reading, *All Joy and No Fun*.

Sure, the mundane and exhausting are punctuated by some pretty tasty rewards. Their faces when they find you in the audience; the funny pictures they draw of you, where you have no ears and one enormous hand; their need to show you the line of cars they made or how they've put pants on all their teddies. These are the advantage points, the business-class air miles you pick up in recognition of your ceaseless loyalty. But Mother Nature isn't stupid. She knows she has to dish out these treats if she's to have any hope of keeping the human race going. Without them we'd probably knock reproduction on the head and, well, we wouldn't be here to find out what happened next.

But one day, just when you are beginning to doubt if even an air-miles trip to the moon could sugar you up this time, you notice the hard labour has eased off slightly. They're probably eight or nine – depends on the child, and your endurance. But there definitely comes a bedtime when you notice that not only have they brushed their own teeth, they did it without even being asked. Tidying their room, you notice that they have fewer toys lying around – it's pretty much just Lego (boys), a secret diary/jewellery-making kit (girls) and a lot of screens (the ones you huff about, but also secretly know you could not live without).

Their weekends are full of activities – football, drama, parties, sleepovers – that don't involve you, beyond driving them there and paying for them – burdens you are more than willing to carry. They don't need you to occupy them. In fact, they'd rather you didn't. Suggest any activity you consider acceptable to your eight-year-old son – read this book, watch this nature documentary, do this word search – and he's all, 'Mum, why would I want to do that?', rolling his eyes like Kevin or Perry (OK, so word searches are pretty dull). But he's still enough of a baby to sob on your shoulder when his little sister pinches him. He can make up songs about his bum that he thinks are so hilarious he can barely get the words out for laughing, but still sleeps over in your room occasionally when he needs a cuddle.

They are good company now, too. Once, a Saturday night at home alone with your daughter was a tightly scheduled series of events leading to bedtime – bath, story, milk. This left you with precisely one hour of your own time to enjoy something with Dominic West in – anything – before you fell asleep on the sofa, like you were in a care home. Now you are happy to eat popcorn and watch *Pitch Perfect 2* with her, and help stage-direct her routines in the living room. You have conversations about the boys in her class and how she is going to split her time between being a vet and designing clothes for pets when she is older. Is it hard being a mum, she wonders? Not at all, you say, and you mean it.

You feel like the CEO of a successful business, who has worked her way up the ranks. Now you're taking more of a consulting role, getting out on the golf course. You are digging on this eight-year-old vibe, man. You wonder why all children can't be eight.

Is Mother Nature up to her old tricks again? You're certainly doing a bit of a Facebook on your own life here – seeing only the good bits. Somehow you seem to be able to overlook the pre-teen strops and high-pitched objections to all hygiene-related tasks. The astonishing thoughtlessness – putting empty juice cartons back in the fridge, leaving the front door open when they leave the house, not flushing the toilet. At times, appearing to not have even reached the toilet and just done it on the floor. And the defiance – oh, the defiance! The *I don't care*s and *OK fine then*s. The slamming doors and horror-movie screaming. The increasing propensity for telling massive whoppers with audacious ease. No, I didn't steal ten pounds from your purse. No, I didn't cut those holes in the leather sofa. Why do you never believe me! Sob, sob, etc. How can you be enjoying it so much, when there's still all this hell to deal with?

Perhaps this is the old girl's way of giving you a power nap. A little calm before the next big storm. Because there is a sense of borrowed time. The dark spectre of the teen-age years looms apocalyptically overhead. Because that is the other thing the old people like to remind you about: the teens are hell. Thanks, old people. Anything else you want to piss all over?

But they're right. You need only talk to any parent of a teen for more than five minutes and you'll recognize the fear in their eyes. It's animal, a look of pure fight-or-flight panic that you haven't seen since the toddler years – an era epitomized for you by that time you took her to the new soft-play centre in town and she did a diarrhoea poo in the ball pit.

So you know this is probably just a short feet-up. You'll be back to some paltry reward scheme soon enough, scratching around for the good bits while they tell you they hate you and wish they'd never been born. But for now, at this moment, as they sit upstairs happily reading a Roald Dahl book in bed, you are really enjoying being their mum.

Acknowledgements

From both of us

A big fat thank you to Elly James, who found our blog and got our jokes and generally made everything happen – what a superstar you are. Also to Heather Holden-Brown at HHB, and to Jack Munnelly for picking us up halfway round the track and helping us reach the finish line. To our publisher, Fenella Bates, who we both have a little style-crush on, and to everyone at Michael Joseph for taking a punt on us. From the very first meeting with the fresh berries and chocolate brownies we knew we were in the best of hands. To our sharp and meticulous editors, Lynn Curtis and Karen Whitlock, who saved us from our sweary, over-sharing selves. To the talented Mr Nicholas Bull, who effortlessly came up with our name when we failed to think of one ourselves. Massive, heartfelt thank yous to all the mums who have provided us with inspiration and insight into the condition we all share. Many of your stories are here in these pages. Apologies also to anyone we may have offended. Especially the men, who we know have their own crap to deal with, but may not moan about it like we do. And extra-special thanks to all those who've read, shared, commented and shouted out about our blog. For all the media brouhaha about women being horrible to each other, we've found that mums really are a nice bunch, the world over.

From Sarah

Thanks to my mum, Thelma Thompson, who still doesn't really know what a blog is, but supports me unquestioningly nonetheless. For bringing home-made soup to hospital, painting every house we've lived in, looking after them while I work and washing up constantly. And for being hilarious, often intentionally. You have set the bar so high. To my dad, Roy, who I miss every day. And to my sisters, Jane Wood and Peta Webb, who keep me on the straight and narrow, and make me cry laughing. Also my brothers-in-law, Tim Wood and Phil Webb – an especially fine pair of uncles. You are all so supportive, thank you. To Tom Woodhouse for being our children's hero. And to Tom's parents, Granny Linda and Grandad Pig, for being such brilliant grandparents. And finally to my beautiful babies, Stanley and Betty Woodhouse. Being your mum is simply the best. I love you both so much.

From Alex

Thanks to my mum, Jan Mattis, for the knitting, the Disneyland trips, the getting up with them, the sympathetic ear, the being amazing when I'm ill, and a thousand more things besides. Any bits of this I get right I learned from you. To my dad, Heber Mattis, for the chats and, together with my aunt Helen, for showing me the funny. To Leslie Kinsey, who travels miles just to help out and always makes the boys' eyes light up. To Derek Manson-Smith for his superlative cooking and for buying me the best books. To my sons, Emilio and Xavier, without whom I'd have no copy, but also no life. You were so longed for, and are so loved. And to Misha, who I love and admire so much, even now we're clocking up close to twenty years. Thanks for your words of reason, your infinite patience, and for being the best all-round life partner a girl could hope for.